Hey Kids,
Start Golf Right!

Hey Kids,
Start Golf Right!

The Foundation for a Lifetime of Success

*a gift from
The Peterkin Family*

JOHN deGARMO
with PGA Professional Sam Wiley

Pentland Press, Inc.
www.pentlandpressusa.com

PUBLISHED BY PENTLAND PRESS, INC.
5122 Bur Oak Circle, Raleigh, North Carolina 27612
United States of America
919-782-0281

ISBN 1-57197-295-1
Library of Congress Control Number: 2001 132265

Printed in the United States of America

DEDICATION

First, to all those Moms who sit, and maybe grab a catnap, or just wait patiently in the parking lot, while the future stars of the game soak up all they can, to be sure they will be stars . . .

And to The First Tee, a wonderful idea that will give thousands of young people the chance to learn "The Greatest Game of All," through its mission of creating affordable and accessible golf facilities for those who ordinarily would not have the opportunity to learn and play the game . . .

Table of Contents

FOR PARENTS ONLY

FOR THE KIDS

Foreword

Let's see. If this book is successful, the child who reads it will grow to love the game of golf intensely. He'll enjoy it, not be afraid of it. She'll respect if, but not sanctify it. He'll know its simple pleasures—a late afternoon round with a buddy as they rush to beat the sunset, a mother-daughter tournament where mom and me take home the fourth flight silver cup . . . but be willing to learn its complicated and uncompromising rules (I mean how can a one-foot putt count the same as a 310-yard drive!?). He'll grow with the game, learning to adjust his expectations to the demands of family and career, but always working to improve because, well, that's three-quarters of the fun. She'll take the game with her on her travels and experience other cultures through the prism of golf. He'll teach the game to his children, share it with his friends, love passing on its lingo and tricks.

In short, if this book is perfectly successful, the child who reads it will grow up to be John deGarmo. John is the author, but he's also the goal: a gentleman, a player, a competitor, a golfer who gives back to his favorite game. John was clever enough to recognize long ago that golf was not only a great sport but great for the spirit. He learned to play it extremely well—John was for years at scratch and is still a low single digit handicapper and helped to shape the several golf clubs he belonged to over the years (now Wee Burn CC in Connecticut and Sawgrass in Florida). He brought home a den full of trophies in the process. While he has deep respect for the game, he's not sanctimonious about it, and certainly not above experimenting with that slightly over-the-limit driver. And he shares his love of the game everyday with friends, like me.

So listen to this voice of John's. It's wise and respectful, but it's full of competitive fire. Just the kind of golfer we all want to grow up to be.

Then there's his friend Sam Wiley, who loves golf and loves teaching it, and loves teaching kids, especially. Which may be why he's so good at it. Or maybe it's because he so thoroughly respects the game. In any case, Sam epitomizes the gentleman-professional. He has that special ability of knowing how to keep it simple, and get the kind of success with his students . . . young and not so young, that makes them happy, successful golfers.

His dedication as an instructor barely exceeds his enthusiasm as a cheerleader. Sam literally lights up when he's working with kids; they are very special to him. And the kids feel it; you can easily tell because they light up too when they're "working" with him.

No matter who he works with, however . . . his talent for teaching works. Take Paul Azinger for instance. Sam was asked to help Paul get back to tour level capabilities after his bout with cancer. Sam got him there. No wonder, considering that Sam has worked with the likes of Craig Harmon, Jim McLean and Dennis Satyshur. What a great way to become a premiere golf instructor. And he's that. Ask Paul Azinger and the kids at Wee Burn; they're proof of it!

BOB CARNEY
Creative Director,
Golf Digest Companies

Preface

Not long ago, as we strolled down a beautiful fairway, my four handicap son asked me, "Pop, how long were you off the tee at your peak?" I quickly said, there wasn't a lot of difference . . . maybe I'd lost a club length over the years.

So what; at my age and stage of golf you don't worry too much what "used to be"; you simply enjoy it . . . even if, as the years sail by, your game way back then keeps getting better than it really was. That's all part of the fun; the mystique that keeps our spirits up as our scores go up too!

The point is that I love golf. The rules and etiquette were every bit as important to developing that love as the work that helped me mature my talents to play the game reasonably well. My respect for those rules and the etiquette have been, I'm positive, as much an influence on my emotions about golf as have my few moments of competitive accomplishment.

The day-to-day enjoyment of having played the game in many countries, with many people has given me volumes of memories, but the most touching part of golf has been the comradeship. It exists among millions of other golfers because here is a game where common courtesy and rigid rules regard, are as much a part of the game as a two foot putt.

Think about this: here's a game you can play with anybody because handicaps allow it to be competitive if you're playing with a beginner kid, or your grandmother—and how about this—you can play it all alone and thoroughly enjoy that too.

There are a lot of young people out there, poised to start the game and have a peak to shoot at . . . just as I am so lucky to have one to look back at.

Introduction

If you're a beginner, you're a beginner. If you've never played golf, and whether you're ten or twenty years old, your knowledge of how to play it is . . . well . . . *zilch*! That could mean this book, while directed at beginner juniors, could help some who aren't juniors but are beginners.

While the Tiger Woods phenomena is credited with much of the explosion of interest in golf, a lot of young people and their families were caught up in the game well before Tiger, and they streamed like lemmings for the nearest available golf course, driving range or family golf center.

This created new opportunities and, frankly, new problems for the game. As for opportunities, think of that beautiful piece of real estate just waiting for someone to build eighteen holes and a club house on it. And, as for problems, think how crowded that eighteen holes has already become on new golf courses throughout the world, not to mention the U.S., where we're building almost one course per day, nationwide.

We're in the age of the "instant golfer." It may be that this book and others written from like perspectives will help eliminate some of the problems the newly anointed golfers cause. Consider the case of the would-be golfer who gets the letter telling him he's now a member of Happy Holes Country Club. He gets up the next day at the crack of dawn. Wife and kids along, he immediately heads for the Pro shop where he outfits the family with Callaway Clubs, FootJoy shoes, Hilfiger shirts and Corbin slacks. They sign up for lessons and, as "instant golfers" step out on the course, take more shots and more time and create more frustrated players behind them than you might think possible.

xiv ᚹ JOHN DEGARMO

I think we should treat these people as *opportunities*, people we can "break in" as players of our future membership by doing everything we can to be sure they do *take the lessons* (some clubs in the U.S. today require players "pass" the Pro before being allowed on the course), *learn the rules,* and *understand the etiquette.* The only rough part here is learning the game, and if the beginners do the other, *learning the rules and etiquette*, then golf's future will be bright and the new golfers will have greater enjoyment in the game.

Let's help get people on the course that have a sincere desire to play the game at least reasonably well, and show the respect for it that has made golf *the greatest game of all.*

I started playing golf when I was just into double digits.

My father wanted me to concentrate on the "skill" shots: bunkers, putting, chipping et cetera. "That," he said, "is where you win it or lose it."

Then there was my godfather, Walter Pedersen. His idea on how to start golf was to concentrate on distance: "whack it hard and far and keep trying that till you can do it. That," he said, "is where you'll win it or lose it."

I learned enough about both their ideas quite fast and won a club Junior Championship by the time I was fourteen. At sixteen a state high school championship, and then, proudly made it to the finals of my club's regular championship . . . only to learn all about "choking." It was quite a lesson.

Played lots of college golf till World War II got in the way.

When that mess was over, back to college, and shortly afterwards into the business world.

It was interesting to me in my naiveté, that golf and business were akin to each other and thus, golf became for me a rather effective selling tool. Then, as now, people who are average or less than average golfers seem to relish playing with people who are right around "scratch."

In those days I read voraciously about the golf swing, the golf masters, and the golf world in general. Played in too many tournaments and never quite became an "item," but I don't regret any of that. I still enjoy thinking about my near misses and blunders.

The author as a junior golfer.

As the world "turned" I got a chance to even coach some high school golf . . . and yes, I learned a lot from that, watching how kids treated adversity and handled good fortune. I had enormous gratification in being able to help them with swing thoughts and the mechanics of the game. This kind of involvement was helpful in my early retirement years when I became involved with the American Junior Golf Association, where I watched and saw emerge such wonderful players as David Duval, Jim Furyk, Tiger Woods, Justin Leonard, and many more.

When I review my life of golf, I realize it is a whole library of learning experiences: the mechanics of hitting a ball of course, but also dealing with the pressures, developing the concentration, reacting to the motivations and perhaps most of all, enjoying the gratification of helping young people who like me, many years ago, aspired to so many goals.

Maybe I'm still a junior golfer.

FOR
PARENTS
ONLY

Some Suggestions Before We Begin

Some of the things you learned to do for your kids, you learned from your parents. And perhaps there are some things you learned from them *not* to do.

What follows are some suggestions that will help your youngster to learn the game and perhaps, more importantly, enjoy the game. More often than not, the two go hand in hand.

Whether you and your spouse are golfers or not is relatively unimportant, though naturally if you are, golf can only strengthen the family bond that exists.

But let's go back to the beginning of getting kids started in the world's greatest game.

Suggestion #1: Obviously you wouldn't try and force 'em into the game. Expose them to golf via the TV, or at a local course or, if you're that fortunate, at your own club. If they are budding stars in other sports, great . . . encourage their enthusiasm for football or basketball, or any sport, just as you would with their golf.

Suggestion #2: Assuming they've shown some interest, perhaps you can find some secondhand clubs, or even purchase new ones. If you play, try and show them, maybe in your backyard, approximately how to swing. Buy a wiffle ball and let them whack it around. Or take them to a golf range or publinx, or better yet, your own club.

Suggestion #3: Think about TV . . . about the opportunity to let them see how it's done, to pick their heroes, to learn the language. And think, too, about how you can be there to have a dialog with them that can be extremely helpful in whetting their golf appetites. This kind of encouragement pays off.

Suggestion #4: In the early years, of say six or eight years old, they're probably too young to caddie . . . but at ten or twelve, they're old enough. The only problem here is that fewer and fewer courses have caddies. But if they do, go talk to the local Professional or in his absence, the caddie master. This might take a little selling to the kid, but that's your job, and we're confident that you can instill in him (or her) the rewards of earning their own money and the bonus of learning the game.

Suggestion #5: A further look at clubs for kids. "Cut-downs" are not ideal, but they're better than nothing. However, local Pro shops may have discards and "starter sets" (they are getting to be a big item in today's growing golf market). Retail outlets have junior starter sets and even "semi-sets." These cost far less than an adult set. They're available at anywhere from $100 up to $300. They consist of a generously lofted driver, perhaps a three wood, three irons, an all purpose wedge and a putter (if you're a golfer you probably have a few putters in your garage, you could even cut one down). And don't overlook those friends you have that have kids a bit older than yours and had starter sets . . . also probably sitting in a garage or upstairs closet.

Suggestion #6: There are golf books that kids can look at, and read and learn from, but usually it's best to get them into books that a club professional would recommend. In the interim, Ben Hogan's *Five Lessons: The Modern Fundamentals of Golf*, has no peer—nobody can miss with that—your kids or YOU! Harvey Penick's *Little Red Book* is the best-selling golf instruction book of all time. It teaches a lot more than golf, but it's all golf related. It's also another opportunity for parent and child to work together. It's easy reading: explicit, simple, and direct.

Book jacket of HARVEY PENICK'S LITTLE RED BOOK by Harvey Penick with Bud Shrake (New York: Simon & Schuster, 1992). Courtesy of Simon & Schuster.

Book cover of FIVE LESSONS: THE MODERN FUNDAMENTALS OF GOLF by Ben Hogan with Herbert Warren Wind (New York: Fireside Books/Simon & Schuster, 1985). Courtesy of Simon & Schuster.

Suggestion #7: Think about a golf school and camps. You can contact those we've listed (see Appendix, p.113), and/or *Golf Magazine* or *Golf Digest* for the golf school ideal for you from a geographical and financial perspective.

. . . And some final thoughts: regardless of whether your youngsters are learning from a club or range professional, or from books, or both, make it your job to *learn what they're learning,* so they can ask you questions and get the answers that aren't too different from their "official" mentor. That way, you can even go to the practice range with them and be some help. If they see you conversing with their instructor, they'll also gain respect for him, which is very important to their confidence.

Another thing—we've touched on matters that have to do with the do's and don'ts of exposing your kids to the game. We can't tell you exactly how to motivate them, but we can tell you that you should try. It won't take them long to realize this is a tough game. It isn't a foul shot or jumping up to snare a pass over the head of the other kid—it's them against the world, and *themselves,* and they need the motivations that you know will work for them. Think about what these may be, by thinking about what they have been in other aspects of their lives, like getting better grades, pleasing their Mom (or Dad), picking up the yard, polishing the car . . . you know what I mean.

. . . and get your PGA Pro involved!

We Asked the Right People Lots of Questions, to Be Sure We'd Help Your Kids

We sought out people who we knew would have the answers to some serious questions about getting kids started *right*.

We developed a questionnaire that was sent to 82 PGA of America (club) golf professionals, 14 NCAA college golf coaches and 66 college players.

Our first question to the professionals asked **what the average age of a beginner-junior golfer was.** *Now* they said it was seven or eight years old—down from about ten just a couple years ago.

This supports the National Golf Foundation, who pointed out that today 17% of beginners are in single digit ages. Why is this? Because TV is there, and Tiger is there, and their peers are there!

We asked the professionals what they felt motivated the kids ·besides TV and Tiger . . . and they said without a doubt . . . parents were number #1 . . . with peers a close second.

We asked our entire panel to give us, in order of importance, **what they felt the most important word on the following list was:**

> *Grip*
> *Rules*
> *Rhythm*
> *Eye on ball*
> *Practice*
> *Etiquette*
> *Concentration*
> *Dress*
> *Motivation*
> *Other*

The top five were: *motivation, grip, stance, rhythm,* and *concentration,* whether it was from professionals, coaches, or college players.

Under *other*, a significant number of respondents said in many different ways, that what may be the most important part of the game was to be sure the kids understood the fun and rewards of the game with friends and family. Amen!

We asked the professionals what was the first thing they taught kids. The overwhelming answer was *safety*. Safety? Yes. If you've seen a lot of kids' clinics you're aware these beginners stand around listening to their instructor tell them how to whack the ball. They know that to hit a ball you have to swing at it, and one of them does just that, and *wham* . . . the kid next to them gets clipped in the back or ear or wherever. Yes, safety is #1.

We asked our college group what motivated them the most. The response was pretty equally divided between:

1) Golf looked like a game that would satisfy their competitive nature.
2) Golf looked like a game that would spark their interest to be the best.
3) They thought it looked tough and wanted to prove they could handle it.

All three points, interestingly, are much the same.

We asked professionals if they felt beginner-kids do better with private lessons or in clinics, and interestingly they felt there was no difference. College kids felt about the same but did point out that clinics were another way to feed the competitive urge . . . interesting . . .

We asked the same groups whether they put emphasis on:

1) The short game
2) The long game
3) Putting

A surprise to us was that putting came in third. Yet when we asked if power or finesse was the most important, finesse won by two to one.

Too many golfers spend too much time trying to hit it *further* instead of spending enough time trying to hit it *closer*.

One of the more interesting questions we asked the college level golfers was **how much time they practiced after a clinic or private lesson.**

ANSWERS: "all day"
"half an hour"
"till I get it."

NOW, THERE'S A MESSAGE . . . additionally, on asking their golf coaches about individual's performances . . . "till I get it" had the best scoring averages.

Arnold Palmer said, "Practice is the only advice that's good for everybody."

Equipment

Look, almost everybody's equipment is good, but there are some out there that we have a better feeling about. For whatever reason, people might just feel a certain confidence in, and therefore play better with, a brand name they're familiar with. And of course, some are simply better than others.

There are today, close to sixty manufacturers of standard golf clubs and balls, that produce equipment for kids as young as, would you believe, three years old? They range from starter sets to the whole shebang.

Be careful; if you aren't pretty sure what's right, seek logical advice. After all, you wouldn't send kids to a school teacher who didn't have the proper credentials, so don't send 'em to learn a great game without the advice of someone with *credentials*—and that's usually a PGA golf professional.

Who's making the best standard equipment now? Going through factories and watching the process and spirit of manufacturers is important in any business. When I came out of the Callaway factory recently, I was pretty confident I'd never play a different brand of club—different strokes for different folks—and I haven't. What would I suggest to my children and grandchildren??????

Obviously, there are others out there that make fine kids' or starter clubs. Taylor-Made is a prime example. And there's of course the great names: Titleist, Ping, and U.S. KIDS. There's even companies that manufacture components like Ralph Maltby's, Golfworks, and Golfsmith.

Regardless of which brand you select for a youngster, be sure to find out if the clubs you're looking at are truly kids' clubs . . .

Are they lighter? . . . Are the shafts more flexible and the correct length? . . . Are the grips a tad thinner? What do they all cost? There's all kinds of prices, dependent of course on quality and whether you buy a starter set of four clubs or six . . . or whatever is available. Generally you'll find sets of four or five clubs with a bag included could run from around $100 to near $300. And most of the companies make it easy to add to the early "brief" sets by making individual clubs from around $20 for the irons, to about $30 for the woods.

One company, Bridgestone, even has a ball with a lower compression which they tell us will give the kids more distance, as will lighter golf balls like the Pinnacle Lady.

I can also suggest a way to avoid prohibitive additional costs early: don't go for all those accessory "frills," e.g., fancy shoes (they can start with sneakers and then the "real thing" becomes a goal). Golf gloves may be fine, but be sure they really need one. Most parents seem to get the idea that if they look like a golfer "early on" they'll be one. A glove won't do it.

I also find too many kids getting into the game, believe it or not, to get into the "awesome" clothes, et cetera and even when they get into them they seem to get peer driven into hats on backwards, and shirts hanging out, and that tells me that someone forgot to tell them about respect for the game. But then that's another story.

Ashworth and Hilfiger, and Polo and Cutter and Buck are great, but they're pricey. Lands' End and L.L. Bean are no slouches for style and color and fit, and they're not so pricey. Remember, clothes aren't going to help their rhythm or smooth their stroke. Besides, if they wear the latter couple of brands they may set the styles instead of following them. Kids like to do that.

Final thought here: what you buy your children or grandchildren to help them learn the game should follow the same kind of thinking that you've probably done yourself, i.e., buy the right thing for the logical purpose, and equally logical price. If you don't try the top of the line right now, you can always upgrade later, perhaps as a reward for progress . . . *think of that as motivation!*

Your PGA Pro will help you here.

A Final Word with Mom and Dad

To begin with, if you weren't already sold on the idea of "junior" golf, you wouldn't even be reading this book, and if the youngster doesn't seem interested in the game, don't even think of forcing it down their throat. They simply dig their heels in, and even if they don't, but play to please you, they're not going to care enough to try as hard as they should. *Golf is a tough game, it takes the very best attitude, without which the very best effort is not possible.*

Until they're "into" the game, don't over burden them with all the paraphernalia. Little kids, in particular, don't need fancy shoes and expensive gloves and a full set of clubs. Get 'em proper "starter" sets . . . and as they move along you can motivate them a bit with a decent pair of *real* golf shoes, and as progress continues, and if their instructor agrees, get them a glove. (Personally, I don't really think gloves are all that important except perhaps in truly hot weather when your hands can slip.)

Don't start right out correcting them on this and that. If, repeat, *if*, you're a single digit handicap, or have been, then your comments will be respected . . . if not, just remember, these are your kids, and they're smart enough to know the importance of "credentials." And if you do play with them (and you should) let 'em know that golf isn't just hitting a ball, and another, and another, and getting a Coke and going home. No . . . it's a sport and it's competition and it's the outdoors, *and it's the enjoyment that goes with all of these.*

And most important encourage your children to get involved in other sports, particularly team sports, where *learning to win and lose as part of a team will help kids learn to cope with winning or losing as an individual.*

FOR THE KIDS

What This Book Will Do, and Won't Do

When you complete this book, and understand more about how to swing a golf club, how to handle the courtesies of the game (*we call that etiquette*) and understand and follow the rules . . . *strictly* . . . you'll be ready to truly start your golf life. Yes, you'll know enough to go to the first tee and *tee it up*.

The advice in this book can help you, but it can't make you a winner. It can equip you to *get a good start*. There are two other ways to help you play golf as well as you want to. The first stems from your own desire and willingness to work at the game—to make that extra effort.

The other is to *see your golf professional*; he's spent a good part of his life training people just like you to play the game just like him; or *better*.

GOOD LUCK!

The harder we work, the luckier we get.
—Vince Lombardi
Coach
World Champion Green Bay Packers

Wonderland

You are about to start on a wonderful journey. It doesn't mean you can't go to McDonalds or play with your Nintendo. It won't stop you from eating M&Ms or running a lemonade stand during the hot weather.

It won't get in the way of football practice, or dancing class, or that movie you're just dying to see . . .

It will give you a chance to meet new friends and learn more about the outdoors and about yourself

The "Wonderland" is called GOLF.

Your journey to it can last all your life and someday in your later years you'll probably take your kids on the same journey—and your grandchildren too!

This journey . . . this . . . *golf* has a magic about it that will feed so many of your emotions. It will sometimes make you happy and sometimes sad, and even mad, but then, just the thrill of it and the new experiences it gives you will be so rewarding.

It will encourage you to try harder and make that trying so worthwhile. It will cause you to have more fun, and closer friendships.

Golf to you will be like space . . . its joys have no end.

Golf is like a roadmap.

You are at a starting point on that map. All you need at this point are clubs and an attitude. If you're going to play the game well, you have to be determined, and your parents have to agree: *"How much time am I going to spend working at this crazy game?"* It will not take many lessons or hours of practice for you to make up your mind if you're "hooked on golf." (And I suspect you may already be leaning that way or you wouldn't have this book.)

There are other influences that also determine that and the main one is your instructor. Perhaps it's your dad or mother who starts you out in the back yard, taking a few swings and then hitting a real ball or even a wiffle ball. Or perhaps it's a golf professional at a nearby range, or your family belongs to a nearby club or there's a public course nearby.

If you start out with a professional instructor, don't, *a million times* don't sign up for one lesson; it's the worst thing you can do. A good instructor will want to talk with you or if it's a clinic, talk with the group to properly initiate you into the game. *And right there could be about half of the time a first lesson should take!*

So plan on a series of lessons. Your Mom or Dad can work that out either with a Pro doing individual lessons or by signing you up in a clinic.

Now, one final word before we get into the mechanics of the game and, depending on your goals, this may be the most important thing in this book:

WHEN YOU START YOUR LESSONS PLAN TO <u>PRACTICE</u> THREE MINUTES FOR EACH MINUTE <u>OF</u> THE LESSON!

That means three thirty minute practice periods for each thirty minute lesson. (Sure it's hard work, but it pays off!) That doesn't all have to be at the range. Sometimes, it's very worthwhile to have a club at home and go into the backyard and practice the action the professional was working on with you. Heck, you can even practice in your bedroom—grab your putter and a glass and a ball, and go to it. (You might even get Mom or Dad into a putting contest in the living room with the same equipment!)

A couple of other points: *your instructor is important*—he's the guy or gal who will start you out on the right foot. He or she is as much a teacher as the one who teaches in your school. You don't have to love 'em, but you <u>do</u> have to listen to them; you have to ask questions, and you want to believe in them. (And you may get to love 'em too!)

One final point: when your instructor says, "OK, Janie (or Jimmy) we're ready for a playing lesson," that's going to be one of the toughest parts of your golf beginnings. That's when you're going to feel pressure for the first time. It may just be a three hole or six hole lesson, but it's important that you give it all you've got—and remember—it's not any easier for your instructor than for you, for they want as much as you do, to see it go well.

GOOD LUCK!

Davis Love said, "You learn golf all the time you play it . . . but you don't learn it all at once."

Let's Go to the Practice Range!

The practice range is where dreams are born. Where youngsters can fantasize about their future conquests on the golf course. Where those dreams can possibly, yes, very possibly, be the beginning of reality.

The practice range has only two purposes: one is to loosen up before you go to the first tee and the other is to learn enough in your beginner days to get you to the first tee *confidently*.

It's where you take your lessons and where you groove what you've been taught. To help you do this we have some suggestions. *These tips will work for you as long as you play golf:*

1) **Whenever you go to practice always have a specific idea of what you want to work on.**

2) **Always loosen up: swing two or three clubs, first baseball bat style, then golf swing style. Even hold a**

couple of clubs behind your back and rotate with the clubs against your shoulders.

3) Remember that the practice range is for golf . . . not for dialogue about movies or TV or the NFL.

4) The quality of your practice is as important as the quantity, but as a rule of thumb . . .

5) after a lesson . . . think about three minutes of practice for every minute of the lesson, though not necessarily all at one time. It may be over the next several days.

6) Don't stay with one club too long. Go from a wedge to a five iron to a driver to a six iron, et cetera, et cetera.

7) Always aim at a specific target: e.g., a tree, a fence post, a rock . . . whatever . . . just aim!

8) Spend as much time chipping and putting as you do on the full shots. After all, you take as many of those shots as you do full ones.

. . . *and someone else will have another tip, and another . . . and you'll think of some too, but most important, remember— practice doesn't make perfect—practice makes permanent; perfect practice makes perfect!*

Let's talk for a moment now about the practice range as a place to loosen up and sharpen up before you play. The majority of people start with a wedge . . . hit a few of those and then several with perhaps the seven iron . . . then with the four iron . . . followed perhaps by a few fairway woods and finally with the driver. Fine, most people do that but that doesn't mean it's the best way to get ready. For example, when you think about it . . . *how often does a player hit three or four or a dozen wedges in a row, or drivers or seven irons, while on the course?* Never! So when you're on the range to loosen up, go ahead with the first club, say the wedge, and hit a few. But after that, go from the wedge to the four iron or a fairway wood, and maybe next to a wedge again. This is much more in keeping with how you'd play the course. What I'm saying I'm sure you understand—play a different club each next shot. Makes sense, doesn't it?

Rex loosens up with shoulder 180s . . .

. . . waist 180s . . .

. . . and some toe touches.

As you finish your warmup routine, imagine the first hole and try a tee shot like you'd hit it, and a second shot like you'd want it, and maybe even a third shot to bolster your confidence.

Mike looks over some "comers."

As a beginner, you'll want to keep alert to learning opportunities. One of the best available, even if you're taking private lessons alone with the professional, is practice range clinics. Doesn't matter if they're four or fourteen people; they can be truly helpful. In addition to learning something, clinics are a great way to strike up friendships, to enjoy competition and to really improve your game, for as the Pro works with you, the others in the clinic will be listening (if they're smart) and so, as he works with others in the clinic, you should listen too. I really can't remember how many times I've been on the range, near a lesson, and heard the Pro tell his pupil something that was a helpful reminder to me.

Your Pro can tell you too!

The 1st Tee:
The Grip

Almost anyone trying to teach golf starts with the grip, goes on to the stance and then to any of several other areas, e.g., *rhythm, concentration, alignment, posture.*

Me? I'm for starting with the grip. The grip is really quite easy and if it's done **right** at the beginning you never need to change it. Put your two hands together, palm to palm. Then simply put them on the shaft, slide one of 'em down, and the other up, and wrap them around the shaft so the club's grip is in the fingers of each hand, and the Vs formed by each thumb and forefinger point between your chin and right shoulder. If you're quite young and have smallish hands, you may want to use the baseball grip; just be sure to have the left thumb (right if you're a left hander) on top of the shaft, and covered by the heel of the right hand. At this point, your left forefinger should be against the right "pinkie" with both of them wrapped around the shaft. *(Let's agree, that from here on, I'm talking about right handers . . . and you left handers just do the opposite, OK?)*

The author says, "If you start with a good grip, you'll never have to change it!"

Palms facing, put 'em up and wrap 'em around the shaft . . .

Ten fingers on the shaft . . . that's called the baseball grip.

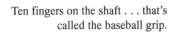

Lock the pinkie of the top hand with the index finger of the bottom hand, and you've got the interlocking grip.

If you're a bit older and can handle it, I'd recommend you use the most common of all grips, the simple overlap. With this grip, the "pinkie" on the right hand goes into the hollow between the forefinger and the middle finger of the other hand.

Here it is at stance . . .

. . . and raised for the Pro to see
if it's right. It's right!

Final thought: there are and can be variations of these grips, but why do it? Keep it simple. There is probably no other aspect of golf tougher to deal with after a couple of years of the wrong grip, than trying to change it. The variations I mention will come later as your game progresses and you need, perhaps, to learn how to draw or fade the ball (Draw is the ball going a bit right to left, fade is just the opposite if you're a right hander, the opposite if you're a left hander).

CHECK THIS WITH YOUR PGA PRO!

The 2nd Tee:

Stance and Address

Getting to the proper stance is step #1 in achieving proper address. All you need to do is stand sideways to the target, with the ball in front of you as if you're going to shake hands with someone on the other side of the ball. Another way to think this . . . it's like you're in the batter's box in baseball. Next, you bend from the hips slightly, flex your knees a bit and let your arms fall naturally. Now you're kind of "sitting down" at the ball. As you start your swing, let your knees move naturally (don't consciously move them), following the rotation of your body as your swing goes back, and the right knee following that rotation as you swing through to the finish.

To control the ball be sure you understand *alignment.* The best image for this is to think of railroad tracks extending from your ball to the target; the near track is parallel slightly left of your target and on your toe line.

Before going to the next tee, let's get one thing very, very clear: *Whatever part of your body moves in your golf swing . . . every part should move together.* For example, as your legs start, so should your hands and hips and shoulders. Only your head stays almost totally still, till after impact, and then it only goes with the flow of your shoulders.

Brianna takes the stance properly, i.e., hips, knees, et cetera . . .

. . . and practices, e.g., "the railroad tracks."

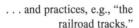

Got that ? *Get it*! . . . and so, let's go to the third tee. But before going to the third tee . . . a question.

How Well Do You "Speak" Golf?

One of the rewards of playing golf is the fun of a whole new language you can learn; it's really just the "jargon" that has emerged from the many people who play the game. Golf has probably more of its own private language than say football which has picked up its "jargon" from non-football events—like "blitz," "bomb" and a bunch of others that we won't get into here—but take a look at these and where necessary, their meaning:

GIMMEE: That's a putt that has been conceded, or "given."

THERE'S A LITTLE CHICKEN LEFT ON THAT BONE: When a long putt has been left too far from the hole to be considered a "gimmee."

YOU'RE ON THE DANCE FLOOR: A playing partner's comment when your ball reaches the green.

KEEP IT IN THE SHORT STUFF: Urging the other player to keep the ball out of the rough.

THAT MIGHT BRING RAIN: When the other guy hits a shot that's obviously way too high.

Some instructional tid-bits:

TEE 'EM HIGH AND LET IT FLY.
GRIP IT AND RIP IT.
SWING EASY-HIT HARD.

Back to the language ones . . .

SPLASHOMATIC: Ball headed towards the water.

HIT A HOUSE!: Your putt is way too firm.

GET LEGS: Putt hit way too easy.

NICE PUTT ALICE: Another way to tell 'em a putt is hit too easily.

LET THE BIG DOG EAT: When it's time to get out the driver—
again.

***NEXT TIME YOU SEE THAT BALL ITS PICTURE WILL BE
ON A MILK CARTON:*** Teeshot really crushed and way out
of bounds.

LIKE IT WAS ON RAILS: Compliment for a straight drive.

TIME TO GET MY RETRIEVER RE-GRIPPED: After the
third time you hit one in the water.

DRIVE FOR SHOW, PUTT FOR DOUGH: The short hitter's
needle after he holes a putt, to win or tie a hole.

RIGHT IN THE HEART!: Comment after a perfect putt in the
center of the cup.

CENTER CUT!: (Same as previous.)

FAIRWAY IS SO TIGHT WE HAD TO WALK SINGLE FILE:
Comment regarding a very narrow fairway.

Good natured complaints from the player hitting a putt that
doesn't drop:

IS THERE REALLY A HOLE THERE?: When he thought it
was in.

WHAT KEPT THAT OUT OF THE HOLE?: Same as above.

THERE'S CELLOPHANE ON TOP OF THAT HOLE: Same
as above.

IT CAN'T BREAK THAT WAY!: Same as above.

THAT ONE GOT CAUGHT IN YOUR SKIRTS: Man's putt left
short.

THAT'S A SOUTH AMERICAN PUTT: Needed one more
revolution.

OUGHT TO HAVE A STEWARDESS ON THAT ONE: Drive
hit way high.

THAT'LL BURN UP ON RE-ENTRY: Same as above.

OK,OK,OK . . . ENOUGH OF THESE . . . ENOUGH!

or

ASK YOUR PGA PRO FOR ANOTHER ONE!

The 3rd Tee:

The Swing

This is where, having learned grip and stance, you start the swing.

Right off the bat, we urge you to start with no more than a half swing. The shorter the path of the club, the surer you are to contact the ball. Chip shots and pitch shots are invaluable in developing a proper impact position. Get your confidence by trying perhaps a whole practice bag this way. Get the feel of contact, get the confidence from contact . . . then take a longer, fuller swing. And by the way, do these swings with let's say a seven iron, or even a nine. Think about it this way . . . *short club, short swing, sure hit.* BUT YOU'VE GOT TO HAVE THE RIGHT "TAKEAWAY" TO HAVE THE RIGHT SWING—SO REMEMBER WHAT WE SAID IN THE 2nd TEE ON STANCE AND ADDRESS and be sure to start your turn with shoulders, hands, arms . . . *everything that moves* . . . working together . . . synchronized!

As your arms come up to horizontal, your hands should raise the club head so that when your hands are just above shoulder level, your left shoulder is pretty near under your chin, and your club is almost parallel to the ground. (But remember this is for the full swing; the half swing, of course starts the same except your hands only get to just above your waist, but they've already started to cock.) Try this—right now—even if you don't have a club handy . . . go ahead, it's easy.

Your main thought or *key* should be that you want to make a proper turn. *What's a proper turn?* That's when, at the top of your back swing, your back is facing the target. Big point here . . . keep your head still. *How do you do this?* Easy, just be sure you have your mind on it and help the mind by using your right leg as a brace that won't let you move your head too much to the right. Letting your head move slightly right is not bad: that's what the tour pros call "loading up." But it must never move up and down—never, and it should never move forward of the ball until after impact; that's how you're going to get a better and *bigger* hit. (Jack Nicklaus says he didn't move his head but he did cock it to the right before starting back. This allowed him the proper "load" and turn.)

Half-swing from the front . . .

. . . and from the side.

Bobby Jones said, "Nobody ever swung a club too slowly."

The 4th Tee:
Driving

There are three types of people in this world:
The ones who make it happen,
The ones who watch it happen,
And the ones who wonder what happened.

—Tommy Lasorda
Manager
World Series Champions, Los Angeles Dodgers

SO, YOUR CLUB IS NEAR PARALLEL TO THE GROUND, AND YOU'RE READY TO WHACK THE BALL!

WHAT DO YOU DO???

Nothing. Well, nothing for a fraction of a second. What you want to do is pause at the top of your swing, literally, just before you're ready to unwind. (Take a swing now, and pause for a whole second . . . just count to one . . . before you bring the club down.) It's surprising how long you feel you've stopped, and another thing . . . it's a great exercise to give you the proper feel of a proper pause at the top.

If you've ever used a slingshot, you know what it's like. You simply "load-up" your spitball, pull back, and *pause.* Heck, you couldn't get the spitball on target without a pause. Then release it! This is the same sequence of motion you use when you throw a ball. One reason kids learn it so well is they imitate the motions they see on TV and even from the driving range where they seem to sense a good swing from one that's not so good.

What that pause really does for you is slow everything down . . . gives your swing rhythm . . . and it should be the same from the driver to the putter . . . *pause . . . pause . . . pause!*

After the pause you're ready to attack the ball. And that will almost come natural; you can't get a car from 0 to 60 mph in a second, you have to depress the accelerator bit by bit. Same with golf. You start to accelerate your arms as soon as you start down. And keep accelerating till *after* you've hit the ball—yes, *after.* That way you're doing what the old time instructors called hitting thru the ball. As you hit through the ball, try to keep the back of your left hand aimed at the target as long as you can. That's about as simple a way to explain how to get club head speed at impact as there is. *Speed will give you distance.*

Now, while on that subject, let me suggest, urge, implore, insist on one thing. As I mentioned above, you must keep your head still. Just as important—keep your eyes focused <u>on the ball</u> . . . yes . . . <u>even on a spot on the ball</u>. I've always looked at the right-most dimples of the ball (except in a bunker shot, but more on that later). I've known instructors that just say focus on the ball. Me? I say *right* on the back or *right*-most dimples. You'll be surprised how much more solid a hit you get that way.

OK, you're about to make contact—now another "key." So, while you may unconsciously have a slight head move to the right with your backswing, you must, repeat <u>must</u>, keep your head dead still as you uncoil . . . *attack* the ball. Part of this is achieved by the suggestion of eyes focused on the ball. Part of it is also achieved, *and* this is very important, by keeping your chest aimed right of the ball—yes, right of it. Think about pointing your belly button to the right; that's a pretty good picture of a swing thought . . . *a key*. Then, as long as you finish the swing . . . there's no way your chest *(belly button!)* will be right of the ball. With a proper and full finish, that belly button will be facing *left* of the target. Yes, left. But let's go to the next TEE and talk about the finish . . .

The author says, "Don't try and hit the kind of shot you think *you should hit, if you can hit one you* know *you can hit."*

Pause . . .

. . . and swing!

See this professional "attack" the ball.

Study Time!

Right now is a good time to think about what you've learned.

What you are learning from your instructor are the fundamental moves made to create a successful golf swing. These are known as "swing thoughts" and "keys." After every few "tees" (chapters) that you go through here, we want you to write down where you've had problems and what you've learned to help eliminate these problems.

The two pages that follow are your "work" area. The first page is for identifying what your <u>problems</u> are, and possible solutions to those problems. Those solutions become your "swing thoughts" or "keys" to improvement. The following page, *"Notes,"* is for other swing thoughts you have, related to these chapters.

These blank pages, once you've filled them out, will be helpful to you as you progress, and several lessons from now, you may again run into a problem and be able to refer back to these pages and *bingo*! . . . there's the problem, and down the page . . . there's the solution!

REPORT CARD #1
The Fundamentals

How well have you done up to here? Grade yourself and see if your instructor agrees. Mark **A, B,** or **C** in each space and you'll know what to work on most.

	I GOT IT!	I'M NOT SURE
GRIP	_____	_____
STANCE and ADDRESS	_____	_____
START of SWING	_____	_____
FINISH of SWING	_____	_____

How Did You Do?

In 25 words or less write down where you consider you may have a problem and what you need to do to overcome it.

(Go to the next page if you wish to make more notes.)

_____

_____

_____

_____

_____

_____

_____

_____   _____
your signature   Instructor's signature
and comments

_____

_____

_____

NOTES

Another Break!

It's time to look at a bit of the funny side of golf, so let me tell you a couple of stories that come from Ireland, where I've visited often and laughed regularly at some of the nicest, warmest, funniest people I've ever known . . . But then you be the judge, here are some of their stories . . .

An American golfer drove into the parking lot at Lahinch, one of Ireland's most famous courses. He was anxious to do better than his round of last year. As he pulled his bag out of the trunk, he noticed his caddie from a year ago approaching him. He greeted the caddie enthusiastically and asked, "Do you remember me from last year?" "Oh, yes sir," said the caddie, "and has your game improved?"

Comment from an Irishman whose two sons had been asked to leave the course for poor conduct, "Tis a poor family that cannot afford one gentleman."

After nearly six hours of hunting lost balls, examining cliffs, taking too many pictures and too many shots, one of the foursome members, at the merciful end of the eighteen hole round, asked the caddie what he owed him, to which the caddie replied, "An apology."

Printed on a score card in the west of Ireland: *A ball may be cleaned and dropped if manure interferes with stroke or stance.*

Irish caddies know the game.

An American golfer in the Pro shop at Ballybunion saw a Footjoy display claiming great benefits for some special kind of new socks. The alert young assistant in the shop asked if he could be of help and answered a couple of the American's questions. Then the American said, "Okay, I'll try a pair." The young man then responded, "Oh sir, customers are only permitted to buy them, not try them."

A visitor to Ballybunion, having hit two terrible shots that left him still short of a brook that really wasn't that far out, asked his caddie, "What'll take me across?" The caddie responded, "There's a bridge right over there."

OK, back to work!

Pointing the way to the most famous courses in Ireland.

The 5th Tee:
The Finish

Have you ever seen anyone finish a shot as gracefully and fully as David Duval?

I haven't . . . don't know anybody who has . . . and yet there is nothing strained about his swing or his finish.

Watch him and you'll see a picture perfect example of getting the right shoulder closer to the target than any other part of his body. His finish . . . *as good as the rest of his game is . . . is one of the reasons he's so straight, and so long.* Notice too that he's practically standing absolutely straight . . . shoulders level . . . and has perfect balance with both feet supporting an almost equal amount of weight, just a bit more on the left leg, as it should be.

This is something you should work at whenever you practice, and with whichever club you're using—look how the young man in the picture on the following page did it, just right.

He's about to make contact—*and here's another "key":* while you may subconsciously have that slight head move to the right with your backswing, you must, repeat *must*, keep your head dead still as you uncoil . . . *attack* the ball. Part of this is achieved by following the suggestion of eyes focused on the ball. Part of it is also achieved, and this is very important, by keeping your chest aimed right of the ball—yes, *right* of it. Think about pointing your belly button to the right; that's a pretty good picture of a swing thought . . . *a key.* Then, as long as you finish the swing, there's no way your chest (*belly button!*) will be right of the ball. With a proper finish that belly button will be facing left of the target.

Will shows you an excellent finish!

This guy has maybe the best of all the finishes . . . nice swing David!

Thanks to photographer Leonard Kamsler for letting me use this "shot."

Now Let's Review!

OK . . . we've said the range is for loosening up and to work on your last lesson's basics.

We've established the <u>grip</u>.
We've mapped out the <u>stance</u>.
Spelled out the <u>takeaway</u>.
Got you into the <u>swing</u>.
And then to the <u>finish</u>.

Up to now we've told you enough about the swing so that you can use this for the majority of shots in the normal round of golf. But then who ever said there was such a thing as a *normal* round of golf? We who play regularly think so anyway. Someone once said, *"<u>How can I be so obsessed with a game that I play so badly?</u>"* Well, that too is part of the fascination.

There have been many big hitters in the game. Names that go so far back they may not even be familiar to your parents. And then there were names you probably know and may even have seen play the game, like Arnold Palmer and Jack Nicklaus.

When Jack came into the game and showed up at The Masters for the first time, Bobby Jones, the greatest of them all (and by the way, very long off the tee) said in regard to Nicklaus' length, "he plays a game with which I am not familiar." And today players like John Daly, considered a monster hitter just three or four years ago, and still long, is not even close to Tiger Woods, and can't keep up with Vijay Singh. But a one-foot putt puts the exact same stroke on the scorecard as a 325-yard drive. And that's where the "skill shots" come into play. If you miss a green and need to get it "up and down" you better be a pretty good pitch shot player. Or deft with a chipping club, or sensitive with a sand wedge. These are the shots most golfers refer to as "skill shots." And before our suggestions on how to play them, I want to tell you that the great players generally spend as much or more time practicing these shots, as they do the drives and fairway woods and long irons.

I've seen Tom Watson, in his prime, hitting thirty-foot chip shots for two hours—yes, hitting from the same spot to the same hole. I've seen Gary Player practice the same length bunker shot for three hours. I even saw him practice pitch shots off a macadam road at St. Andrews for 45 minutes preceding "The Open" over there, back in the mid-80s.

Golf is work. Golf is discipline. Golf is wonderful!

The 6th Tee:
Short Sand Shots

The greenside bunker shot, out of sand, is the easiest shot in golf. Yes, the easiest! You don't even have to hit the ball! The entire objective is to get it out onto the green and leave yourself a makeable putt. What's so hard about that? OK, let me put this another way. This is a shot which requires some finesse; "touch." But with a fair amount of practice it isn't that difficult. I consider myself an excellent bunker player. Half the reason I'm good at it is *I think* I'm good at it and yes, I worked at it in my early years and still hit a few practice shots every few rounds.

You look at a spot behind the ball and aim for that. And with a proper swing you'll have yourself a makeable putt. Just practice it enough to develop that "touch" I talked about above. Forget the tale that bunkers are terrifying. Just find a practice method and get your Pro's input.

How do I *think* about my bunker shots?

OK, first I have an open stance . . . maybe 30 degrees . . . but even that depends on how far the flag is from the position of my shot; e.g., if I've got a 70 or 80 foot shot I'll have the face dead square and even my stance less open. But let's stick with the average bunker shot, which is probably between 25 and 35 feet.

I try and visualize sliding the blade of my wedge under the ball; my stance as I said is open, with slightly more weight on my left leg than right. And I want to take the club back in the same line as my body is set up, which means I will probably be swinging across the line from ball to flag—fine.

I try and hit about an inch or, at the most, two inches behind the ball, dependent on the condition of the sand. Usually an inch behind is fine. I don't buy that bit I've seen recommended, about two inches behind the ball; if you did that chances are you'd have to hit it again from the sand. The main change I make based on wanting more or less distance, is the speed of my arms on descent. I may also change the degree the face is open based on the distance, as mentioned above; e.g., long shot, less open . . . short shot, more open—pure logic. Most importantly, keep your swing going through the ball, and stay loose!

A good image is to try and let the club "throw" sand out of the bunker and onto the green. The ball will follow if you finish the swing.

Your PGA Pro can fine tune you.

Take the club back, slightly outside the line . . .

. . . "slide" the blade under the ball . . .

. . . and swing *through* the ball.

The 7th Tee:
The Long Sand Shot

This is obviously quite a different kettle of fish. To begin with, this shot is much more like your regular fairway shot—that means you should contact the ball before you hit the sand. It also means you should, first of all, be sure you have a solid stance ... dig your feet into the sand, with perhaps a touch more weight on your left side than on a regular greenside bunker shot. IMPORTANT HERE: choke down the club just a bit to compensate for the depth of your feet in the sand. When you do this it shortens the arc of the swing and therefore the flight of the ball will be slightly less than you normally get for the seven iron or four iron that you're using. So, go with one more club . . . like the six iron or the three iron.

This can also be helpful in that it will prevent you from trying to hit the ball too hard; you'll maintain your balance better and you'll more than likely make sharper contact.

There is one school of thought that says you should open the stance up a bit, and I like this as long as I've put the ball slightly back in my stance. I also try on any long sand shots to keep as still as possible from the waste down to assure clean contact.

One other thing I do is, rather than look at the back of the ball, I focus on the top of the ball to try and assure clean contact. As long as you stay still over the ball and during the swing, this should work for you.

SPECIAL SAND SITUATIONS

I mentioned earlier in this "sand section" that the bunker shot is the easiest there is—that you don't even have to hit the ball. In some cases you shouldn't hit the ball; e.g., with a buried lie you simply square the face and take a whack at a spot maybe half an inch behind the ball with a pretty standard swing. Be sure not to try and take the clubhead past the ball; leave it *right in the sand.* There isn't any way to really teach you more than method on these pages, so get in a bunker, bury a ball and give it a try. And another and another. You'll quickly see that from a buried or "embedded" lie, the ball tends to roll further. This is another shot that we classify as a "touch" shot.

OK . . . On uphill sand shots, you have two things to learn. First, try and get your shoulders parallel to the angle of the sand where your ball is and take an almost normal swing. I say almost only because I want you to be sure to be slightly more aggressive than normal. What is *"slightly more aggressive?"* We're back to "feel" or "touch." A bit of practice on this shot will give you the necessary "touch."

OK, up to now the sand shot has been easy; the downhill sand shot isn't. Not by a long shot, but I can make it easier for you if you'll "listen" carefully . . . and then do what? Practice it!

OK . . . when you get over the ball and take your stance be sure your shoulders are parallel to the contour of the bunker at the point where you're set up. That means, of course, your spine is perpendicular to the contour, and therefore the majority of your weight will be on your left side. So, now you're ready to take your swing and things get back to almost normal. With an almost square face try once again to simply slide the club head under the ball, being sure to hit through the ball—remembering, however, that downhill sand shots run a little more than shots from a level lie.

One final piece of advice: on a downhill shot you may have to cock your wrists a bit earlier to avoid touching the sand on your backswing, and you may have to release a bit earlier but keeping the clubhead parallel to the slope of the sand. Nick Faldo calls this move "chasing" the ball—nice description.

The author says, "The best way to lower your handicap fast is to spend a couple of hours in a bunker . . . practicing."

So now you're at the green . . .

REPORT CARD #2
The "Skills Shots"

How well have you done with these?
Once again, grade yourself: A, B, or C.

	I GOT IT!	I'M NOT SURE
SHORT SAND SHOTS	_____	_____
LONG SAND SHOTS	_____	_____
PITCH SHOTS	_____	_____
CHIP SHOTS	_____	_____
PUTTING	_____	_____

How Did You Do?

Your comments: _____

_____

_____

_____

_____

_____

_____

_____

(go to next page if you need more room)

_____   _____

your signature   Instructor's signature
and comments

_____

_____

_____

NOTES

The 8th Tee:
Junior Programs

Good things happen to those who hustle.
—Chuck Knoll
Coach
Superbowl Champions, Pittsburgh Steelers

What kind of junior program does your club have?
KIDS . . . SHOW THIS TO YOUR PROFESSIONAL!

As junior golf continues to grow by leaps and bounds, more and more clubs are developing programs that help juniors to not just play the game, but also to enjoy the excitement and gratification of group participation, competition and the rewards of both.

Obviously the most successful programs are those that are carefully planned and orchestrated.

Mike Krick was an assistant Professional at Wee Burn Country Club in Darien, Connecticut and today is a head Pro at Carolina Trace, in Sanford, North Carolina. While at Wee Burn he developed a program for Wee Burn's young folks that covered most of the bases.

Perhaps the key ingredient of the program was Mike's enthusiasm and resultant capability at working with kids. Also important was that he didn't try and change everything that the previous Professional in charge of the Junior program had started; he worked with it and learned from it. Mike had another advantage; his wife is also a golf professional.

Mike put his successful program together with three ideas in mind: get the kids to practice hard, get 'em to feel the excitement of competition and most importantly, be sure they enjoy themselves.

The first "item" in his program was a "Player Agreement."
Serious stuff. It obligated the players to recognize the game's
values, specifically: *be sure to be courteous and polite, be sure to
show you have self control, be sure to show respect for your
fellow player and/or competitor, and be sure to show that same
respect for the golf course.*

What this "Player Agreement" did was set a serious tone for
the program. The kids felt Mike was serious about helping them,
and he supported that feeling by presenting each of them with a
total program.

It consisted of :

1. A complete schedule of the summer's clinics; you could
   sign up for a three week clinic or a six week clinic; each
   clinic consisted of two weekly sessions.

1998 SCHEDULE OF EVENTS

DIVISION DATE	TIGER WOOD'S DIVISION	DAVID DUVAL'S DIVISION	NANCY LOPEZ'S DIVISION
MAY 19	Putting Elimination Contest	Chipping Bull's Eye Contest	Driving Hit at Balloons Contest
MAY 25	Driving Hit at Balloons Contest	Putting Elimination Contest	Chipping Bull's Eye Contest
JUNE 2	Chipping Bull's Eye Contest	Driving Hit at Balloons Contest	Putting Elimination Contest
JUNE 9	NO CONTEST DAY. Trip to Westchester at 4:00. Points will be awarded for attendance only at Westchester, or you can still come to the Wee Burn Clinic at 4:30–5:30.		
JUNE 16	Driving Baseball Bat Homerun Contest	Putting Big Circle Contest	Pitching Most on Green Contest
JUNE 23	Pitching Most on Green Contest	Driving Baseball Bat Homerun Contest	Putting Big Circle Contest

2. The schedule specified what each clinic would be about. For instance, the first was about RULES AND DEFINITIONS, a most serious, but too often overlooked beginning for junior golfers (older beginners too!)

JUNIOR SUMMER PROGRAM

GOAL: JUNIORS TO LEARN GOLF RULES, DEFINITION AND SWING FUNDAMENTALS.

EACH WEEK A NEW DEFINITION AND RULE WILL BE PRESENTED TO THE JUNIORS. DURING THE FOURTH WEEK A TEST TO MATCH WORDS WITH DEFINITIONS WILL BE GIVEN. DURING THE LAST WEEK A FINAL TEST WILL BE GIVEN TO MATCH WORDS WITH DEFINITIONS.

JUNIOR BUCKS

"JUNIOR BUCKS" CAN BE EARNED AND USED FOR PRO SHOP MERCHANDISE. THEY CAN BE USED TO BUY CLUBS, BALLS, GLOVES, SHOES AND MORE!!!

---

3. Each player received a rules sheet and then a list of definitions: e.g., what's a teeing ground, a bunker, a hazard, a provisional ball, out of bounds, et cetera. With each definition, the specific rule related to the definition. This segment was incidentally reviewed from time to time throughout the weeks of the clinic.

4. Mike ended this kind of "study period" on a high note by demonstrating some shots, explaining facts related to distance and trajectory and really getting his "kids" off to a fast and exciting start.

5. "Junior Bucks" (funny money): now there was a winner! The kids could earn "bucks" through their good sportsmanship, attendance, rules test results, progress with "the game" and attitude. The "bucks" they earned could be

used for Pro shop credit! This was an extremely successful idea which had motivational benefits in just about every aspect of the clinic program.

6. Then there were leader boards. These were sheets displayed at every clinic that stimulated, very gently, a spirit of competition, by showing which of the youngsters were earning "bucks" and in what category.

JUNIOR AWARDS

AWARDS	WINNER
Junior Club 13 & Older	Jed Johnson
Runner-Up	Patrick Moore
Junior Club Champion 12 & Under	Jay Peters
Runner-Up	Kevin Peters
Girl's Junior Club Champion	Rebecca Robbins
Runner-Up	Mary Robbins
Most Valuable Player	Will Culbertson
Most Improved	Bill Peters
Pro's Award	Brooke Gilbert
Most Dedicated	Nik Montgelas

At the conclusion of both the three week and six-week clinic, Mike held an awards presentation honoring the winners of bucks: the champions and runners up for both boys and girls and in two age brackets (ten and under and eleven and over). There were also awards for Most Valuable Player. These were, of course, for that boy and girl who'd advanced enough to participate in inter-club competitions, and displayed their talents and contributions enough to be considered "MVP."

There were some parents that were concerned that those who hadn't made the team might be discouraged, but Mike told us he found that overwhelming majority who hadn't made the team seemed even more motivated to work that much harder to be sure they made it next time.

There were also instances where kids had signed up for a three week clinic, didn't make the grade as a player, and pleaded to get another three weeks . . . and usually did . . . and it usually worked.

It is from such programs as these that America's next champions will emerge—whether it's in golf or in just being a nice well rounded, happy citizen.

Your PGA Pro can do this for you.
BE SURE HE SEES THIS SECTION.

The 9th Tee:
Pitching and Chipping

THE MAN WHO CAN PITCH AND CHIP WELL IS THE MAN WHO'LL WIN MOST OFTEN . . . *BET ON IT!*

The PGA Tour's top players, with rare exception, average hitting more than a dozen greens a round over the span of one tournament. There are times when they hit six greens, but if their pitch and chip shots are accurate they might well break 70.

In the putting section of the book we talk more philosophically than <u>physically</u>—more about thinking than about the physical act of hitting the ball. That's because putting is so much more a mind game in which you must work on the basics and once you've got them, have the confidence to go ahead and stroke the ball.

When you get to the putting section (next "tee"), three points:

1. still head
2. low stroke
3. eyes on a spot on the ball, and keep 'em at that point till the ball has left the blade.

And that's what your chip shot should be—it's a putting stroke with a lofted club. What loft? Whatever loft it requires to get the ball just to the green, so it can roll most of the way to the hole. As you practice it, you will get a "feel" for this important shot.

When you get to a longer chip or pitch shot . . . say ten to twenty yards from the green to a flag well back . . . it's easier for most players to open their stance a bit, and let their hands come *quietly, gently* into play. The length of the shot will determine the length of your swing and how much you use your hands.

I got a tip years ago about hand use on pitch shots from a teaching professional friend of mine: he said that if you were close to a green, you might throw a ball onto it with an underhand "pitch" motion, but as you went further from the green you thought you needed to go to a regular overhand motion . . . it's at that point that you start to use your hands.

Good thing about this shot is that it's a bridge between the "chip-putt" style I advocate above, and the regular pitch shot. The regular pitch shot is dependent upon your swing. Time, talent and experience will tell you much more than I can. Go out and try it; have fun getting better each time you practice it.

Keep in mind, the pitch shot will have even more wrist action—more like a normal swing—though rarely as much.

You'll find that on short pitch shots it's more natural to have your feet, hips and hands slightly "open" and as the shot gets longer, you simply get more square to your target. There's nothing fancy here . . . much of it comes naturally—let it happen.

Chipping

Here's Greg. He takes it back, just like a putt . . . nice and
slow . . . and low, and goes through it just like a putt . . . low,
being sure to accelerate through the ball.

Pitching

And here's Will. Same idea as Greg, above . . .
just a little longer shot so a little longer swing.

The 10th Tee:
Putting

WE THINK PUTTING WILL FORGIVE MOST SINS. When a player hits big drive after big drive, OK . . . you kind of expect him to keep doing it. But when that same player sinks big putt after big putt, that gets spectacular.

Do you know that Payne Stewart is the only U.S. Open Champion who won that event by sinking a lengthy putt on the final hole of regulation? And there have been over one hundred U.S. Opens!

Did you know that Ben Hogan was literally driven from competitive golf because of his putting woes? And Johnny Miller, the guy most of us know as a great broadcaster, the same.

There are two, and maybe you can stretch it to three, basic golf grips for normal shots. For putting? Oh my . . . baseball grip (there are two), Vardon grip, and interlocking grip with one or two or three fingers. And then the reverse interlock, then the latest grip which is referred to as "left hand low" but, when started, was just called "reverse grip."

How come all these grips? And then how about the many weights and styles of putters that have been born of frustration? There are more I suspect than anyone can possibly count. Many have been ruled illegal, e.g., the Schenectady putter of the late 20s and early 30s, used by such greats as Hagen and Sarazen and untold others. Then along came the long putter which helped people straddle the ball croquet style . . . soon that was ruled illegal. Then its cousin for side straddling the ball came out. It created a bit of a "war" when some of the officials of golf thought it too should be ruled illegal. But that hasn't happened . . . yet. And it probably never will.

You might wonder why all this talk about a club, instead of a swing. *It's because putting is the most difficult of all strokes to do well, consistently.* And actually that's not hard to understand because it is first, the swing that is the most delicate and secondly, it has less margin for error when you realize its target isn't even five inches wide, while with a driver you often have a target that's forty yards wide! It's probably fair to say that the better golfers spend more time on putting than on almost any other club. It is the one of two clubs in the bag (the other being the driver) that is probably used in every practice or warm-up session.

That's because these two clubs are the two that can keep you in more competitions—or put you out of them—than any other in the bag. I think the putter is the most important. It is also the one that seems over the years to have caused more pressure than any other club. In a grueling final few holes you rarely see a truly bad drive or iron shot, or even bunker shot. But how many putts do you see pushed or pulled or simply not solidly hit?

Why? Pressure. Why? Because too many of us are thinking about the outcome rather than about the fundamentals we've been taught; e.g., head still, club low, eye on ball, et cetera, et cetera, et cetera.

Too many of us change our routine when the pressure is on a bit.

Too many of us think more about "can we make it?" rather than how we're going to make it.

Too many of us get an idea of the line, and don't really commit to it, i.e., do we not infrequently change our intended line in mid stroke? *Yes in mid stroke . . . would you believe it?*

The only additional thought I'll offer here is you're learning to putt all the time. Sometimes you putt better than others (same with your driver or wedges too) but sometimes things go way off. Keep doing what you're doing for a round or two and if you don't get over your problem, then try something radically different. That may work for a round or two. If it does, keep with it. When it backfires on you, go back to the "old" way; I'll bet it works.

We're not going to get into speed and break of greens here. Your professional can get you started properly on that, for he's on hand, and these two points are more "touch" than mechanics. When you've learned to putt fairly well you'll probably think of putting as purely touch—and so you should. What we're going to leave you with is this:

DON'T GET AWAY FROM THESE FUNDAMENTALS:

1) **Keep your head and shoulders still, stroke with your shoulders, not your hands (note PGA Tour Champion Jeff Maggert).**

2) **Keep your stroke low, back and then through the ball (note PGA Tour Champion Phil Mickelson).**

3) **Keep your eyes on a spot on the ball, and don't move your head to follow it till well after the ball has left your blade (note PGA Tour Champion Tiger Woods).**

CHALLENGE A FRIEND!
CHALLENGE YOUR PRO!

You know Will came through low by how straight his arms are . . .

The practice putting green is an important part of the practice "range."

The 11th Tee:
Tips for the Course

For medal score: Don't gamble; lose a shot but *advance the ball*; a one-putt green can make up for the "safety play." A gamble can cost too much.

In match play: When you win a hole, try harder to win the next one too, and the next. Get the match over quickly as possible.

In match play: Gamble only *when you need to,* your opponents position on the hole may dictate your shot. *Think hard!*

Re "swing keys": Don't listen to the turkeys who say "don't think, just swing," or the ones that tell you to "think of one thing only." There's nothing wrong with having a couple of "keys" on a shot; e.g., one getting you back, one getting you down.

About water: If water is in play from the tee, and it's to your right, tee up on the right and hit away from it. If it's on the left, do just the opposite.

About the "waggle": It's a good tension reliever and it's good for your rhythm. If you use it on the course, use it on the range—after all, the range is preparing you for the course.

A buried sand lie: If it's real deep, use a pitching wedge and play it the same as you'd play the sand wedge.

A really long greenside bunker shot: If you've got 60 or 70 feet to go and plenty of green between you and the hole, think about using your pitching wedge and hitting a pitch-type shot.

Playing in wind: Hit it hard downwind and easy into the wind.

Don't fret: If you've hit a bad shot, and you will, forget about it and think about the next shot.

About nerves: Everybody gets nervous, regardless of age or experience. When you get nervous, whether it's for the "Tee Wee Club" Championship or the U.S. Open, just go back to fundamentals. It will help.

The power of thought: It doesn't always work but it usually does; e.g., if you need a slight fade then think *fade.* If you need a slight draw, think *draw.*

For better chipping: Watch some of the pros in a tournament. When they're quite near the green and don't want to putt, they take a six or seven iron and chip it *with a putting stroke.* This is also good when you've been having problems with your chipping.

Uphill lies: Get your spine perpendicular to the ground, and use one extra club. The ball should be a couple of inches forward, and then use a normal swing. The tendency is for the ball to be pulled to the left for right handers.

Downhill lies: Get your spine perpendicular to the ground, use one less club. The ball should be a couple of inches back, and then a use normal swing. The tendency is for the golfer to be slightly ahead of the ball which causes a push.

Practice: Practice your putting more than anything else !

IF YOU WANT TO BE EXTRA GOOD, GO THE EXTRA MILE!

Ask your PGA Pro for *his* top tip!

The 12th Tee:
Advice

To all of you who've worked your way to this part of the book and feel you've learned something, let me quote a famous English golfer who wrote something most reasonably good golfers believe:

> **I have told you repeatedly that you must develop your own style, and while I have described some of my own methods, I repeat that you must not necessarily follow them except in general principle. By this time you may know sufficient about the game to be able to make experiments for yourself. Try to form your own style, remembering that it is the work you do yourself that will help you to become a good**

> **golfer. Hints and tips from others may be useful at times, but more often than not these work only for a few days. If you work out your own game on the lines I've suggested, you will soon discover for yourself what is useful to you and what is not. But it is only hard work—disheartening work, sometimes—that can make you the player you would wish to be.**

Photo provided by
Golf World

—Henry Cotton,
British Open Champion, 1934, 1937

<u>Charles Blair Macdonald</u>, who lived until 1927, spent his teen years in college at St. Andrews, Scotland, and thus was introduced to golf at age sixteen, far earlier than most American youth.

He wrote a book, published in the late 20s, in which he said:

> **The earlier rules of play always suggested a code of honor. One rule alone governed the play after driving off; the player must play the ball as it lay and not interfere with his opponent's ball. The ball was not to be touched with anything but a club until it was holed out. There were only two exceptions—a lost ball or a ball in water. In each case there was a penalty.**

He later mentions that the influence of his association with St. Andrews was so strong that to touch a ball in play was like a religious profanity to him.

Macdonald was from Chicago and returned there after his college years. There wasn't a golf course in America then, but that ended that year, 1892, when Macdonald built the first one. He went on to build many courses and play a great deal of golf.

He was an energetic, innovative, rambunctious and even egomaniacal man, yet when all was said and done . . . and I quote the greatest golf writer of the 20th century, Herbert Warren Wind . . . "no one had a comparable influence on *the development of the game in this country.*"

Charles Blair Macdonald
Photo provided by *Golf World*

Another man, who one prefers to really call "gentleman" was Bobby Jones. He established competitive goals that have stood for more than seventy years, but more important he established a mantle of such enormous respect and love for himself by the Scots that they invited him there in 1957 to receive from the Provost of the town of St. Andrews, the keys to the city. This honor had never before, nor has it since, been bestowed upon an American. He had his way of showing his hosts his enormous appreciation, when at the presentation, though now a seriously crippled man, he discarded his crutches and acceptance speech notes, and said to the assembled throng, "If I were to take from my life all my experiences but those in St. Andrews, I would have had a full and gratifying life."

Those gathered who heard the words stood and as though led by a choirmaster (though they weren't) sang a Scottish song, "Will ye no comeback again . . ."

Which of course Jones never did, he died just a few years later.

I tell you these stories about three entirely different personalities, who made their mark in golf at totally different times. Each was so respectful of the game and the *influence its*

Bobby Jones
Photo provided by *Golf World*

rules caused, that they have influenced newcomers to the game to maintain that same respect, and the rigid standards of integrity that make the game *the only one of its kind.*

I have put these thoughts here, proceeding the sections on Rules and Etiquette, because the three men I've briefly profiled are such wonderful examples of the spirit of the game. It is that spirit of integrity and courtesy which we hope will keep the rules rigid, and the etiquette constant.

And that's up to you.

ASK ANY GOLFER!

ESPECIALLY YOUR PGA PRO!

The 13th Tee:
Etiquette

The USGA (United States Golf Association) protects the integrity of the game. In *The Rules of Golf*, the book which spells out all the rules and definitions, the first subject they cover is etiquette. That tells you how important they feel etiquette is.

The dictionary says etiquette is *conduct required by good breeding.*

Arnold Palmer says etiquette means *treat other players the way you'd like to be treated*

Snoopy says *good golf course etiquette makes golf a better game.*

Sawgrass Country Club says *more care, more course, more fast, more fun.*

BUT WHERE DOES IT ALL START?

It starts on the practice range.

Up front of this book we mentioned the research we'd done to put this "teacher" together. In that research we learned that of 82 responses from the professionals only two of them said they did not discuss *dress* with their students.

Dress is a significant part of etiquette, because dress relates to conduct.

Paul Leslie is today the head Professional at New Canaan Country Club, in New Canaan, Connecticut. Prior to his appointment there he spent five years at Wee Burn Country Club in the next town, Darien.

As a "beginner" professional, he was given the assignment of handling the Junior clinics, which he decided immediately should be "programs." Among the several parts of his program one segment was devoted to "dress" because dress, Paul felt, says something about attitude, and attitude is a major factor in developing any kind of talent.

On the opening day of Wee Burn's Junior program, Paul headed for the back of the driving range, blew a whistle, and about forty, eight- to fourteen-year-old, excited boys and girls, clamored for a "front row" spot.

Now Wee Burn isn't exactly a blue collar club and on occasion has been considered perhaps a bit stuffy, and the kids with their Polo's and Hilfiger's and Nike caps kind of reflect that.

Paul waited patiently at the front of the group till the giggling and talking settled down, then said "Good morning" and after a slight pause, in a most upbeat and quiet voice, "OK, my friends, welcome to our Wee Burn Junior series. Today we start our clinics to teach you about *the game of golf.*" Then, suddenly, his voice got stronger as he said in an almost booming tone, "Put your hats on, brim forward and tuck in your shirts. And that my friends, is lesson number one!"

After a moment the surprised kids stopped mumbling and grumbling, and straightened their caps, tucked in their shirts, and stood a little straighter. Paul then told them of his love and respect for the game and urged them to give golf a chance and maybe someday "you'll feel as I do."

This may have been the most successful junior program ever held at Wee Burn up to that year. And it might interest you to know that the young assistant Pro who followed Paul when he left for New Canaan continued much of Paul's program, and expounded on it to the great benefit of the kids. He also made sure that hats were on bill front, and shirts tucked in.

The reemphasis on etiquette in very recent years has happened because golf's incredible growth has left a few folks out there without the basic knowledge of not just how to hit a golf ball but also how to conduct one's self on the golf course. That's not easy unless someone helps you, by showing you and telling you, so we're going to try to do just that.

The hat on the left is being worn correctly,
while the hat on the right is worn incorrectly.

Shirttails should always be worn tucked in on the golf course.

1) BE CAREFUL! Never swing a club if there is anyone near you. Look around before you swing.

2) Don't talk, and do stand still when another member is about to hit. Try to always stand facing the hitter, out of their line of sight.

3) Keep up with the players ahead of you, stay ahead of the players behind you.

4) Remember, if you need more than one practice swing, excluding those times when in an unusual topographical situation, such as against a bush or on an unusually steep grade, et cetera, the second one isn't going to help.

5) If you're off the fairway and can't find your ball in three minutes, it's time to "reload."

6) If you have to survey a putt like you're Tiger Woods, and your name isn't Tiger Woods, don't do it.

7) Estimate your distance from a yardage marker; don't spend a lot of time walking off the distance.

8) Be ready to hit when it's your turn.

9) Be ready to putt when it's your turn. (Line up the break while the others are putting).

10) Think of yourself as longer than you are and you won't hit anyone in front of you.

11) Start planning your next shot as soon as you've hit your last one.

12) Replace your divots or refill them with sand.

13) Replace other players divots when they don't . . . and do the same with ball marks on the greens and footprints in the sand.

14) When on the green, be careful and don't walk on the other person's line.

15) If you're keeping score, do it on the next tee, not the green you just played.

16) Keep your ball in sight till it stops, and you'll save a lot of everybody's time. (Keep their ball in sight too.)

17) Don't throw clubs—EVER!

SPECIAL TO THOSE WITH GOLF CART TRANSPORTATION

1) If you're on "cart paths only" take two or three clubs with you to your ball, if you're in doubt.

2) Drive a golf cart between the green you're playing and the next tee and never, repeat *never*, within specified distances from greens and tees.

3) If your group is holding people up—let 'em through, you'll both enjoy the day more.

Finally, leave the course in better condition than you found it, treat everyone on the course the way you'd like to be treated and

BE A ROLE MODEL!

The 14th Tee:
Things to Remember

Introducing the Kennedy twins, Will and Greg,
and their presentation of a few things to
remember on the course.

When your playing partner is hitting the ball, stand facing him (her), stand
still, and follow the flight of the ball. (We don't want to lose it!)

When you rake a bunker don't leave ridges caused by careless raking.
You wouldn't like them!

Never walk across your playing partner's putting line.
Set an example for her or him.

Be sure to hold the pin, flag to the ground, and out of sight of your partner.
(And if you're tall enough, and the wind is blowing,
hold the flag to keep it from blowing around.)

When the hole is over, replace the pin carefully,
so as not to damage the side of the cup.

The 15th Tee:
Golf Organizations

A GOOD YOUNG GOLFER WITH A GOOD ATTITUDE AND GOOD GRADES CAN GET A GREAT EDUCATION.

There are four national golf organizations that can help juniors with their game, and in some cases with their future. The most prominent is of course, the <u>United States Golf Association</u>. They oversee the rules of golf, producing an annual booklet that carries the name *The Rules of Golf,* plus the date the booklet is in effect. They also produce a booklet, *Golf Rules in Brief*, part of which is reprinted later in this book.

In their efforts to help maintain the integrity of the game, they work in consort with the Royal and Ancient Golf Club of St. Andrews, Scotland, as well as other nation's golfing organizations.

You will see later in this book, several of the rules that are particularly important for the beginner to be aware of. We urge that as you start to play more, you be sure to request from the USGA their booklet.

They have a junior membership for $15 for which you get a year's subscription to the Association's magazine, *Golf Journal*. It is "homey," nicely written, carries some good stories, good reviews of their events, rules questions and is really quite enjoyable. Other "goodies" include a "feel-good" bag tag, product discounts (they have their own catalog of top brand merchandise), decals, et cetera. They also have their headquarters "Golf House," in Far Hills, New Jersey where visitors are welcome to their well done museum (it's worth the trip).

If you want to contact them, write:
USGA
Box 508
Far Hills, New Jersey 07931-0708
Or you can phone them at:
1-800-223-0041

The USGA conducts several national championships every year. They are inevitably the ultimate tournament in their category, e.g., U.S. Open tournament, Mens' and Ladies' categories; National Amateur tournament, Boys' and Girls' categories . . . and so on.

The **PGA of America** is the governing body of club Professionals. There are 45 regions in the U.S. and each has an executive director who conducts events for the "local" professionals, and oversees what is a growing list of junior events. To reach your local region, in case you don't know where it's located,

Call the national headquarters at:
1-561-624-8400
Or write to:
PGA OF AMERICA
100 Avenue of Champions
Palm Beach Garden, FL 33418

By the way, they are adjacent to the PGA National golf club which boasts three golf courses and a residential community which is, of course, very golf oriented.

They conduct the PGA Junior Series for girls and boys, 13 to 18 years old. It includes 12 events from June till August; the cost is $40 for 36-hole events and $60 for 54-hole events.

The <u>Ladies Professional Golf Association</u>, along with the USGA and the Girl Scouts of America, administer the LPGA Girls Golf Club for girls from ages seven to seventeen. They have 97 locations around the world. Membership costs vary according to location, but range from $7 to $15. The girls get a kit with a membership card that admits them to LPGA events and, of course, the usual bag tag and a subscription to the *LPGA Golf Magazine*, which is good, and should be, since it is published by *Golf Magazine*.

They have a wonderful program called the Crayola LPGA Tour, Junior Golf Clinic Program. Clinics are held at 18 LPGA events around the country and have "hands-on" involvement of LPGA tour players.

You can write them at:
LPGA
100 International Golf Drive
Daytona Beach, FL 32124-1092
Or call:
1-904-274-2600

GIVE THIS NEXT ONE SPECIAL ATTENTION!

The <u>American Junior Golf Association</u> is about twenty five years old. It is dedicated to not only creating great events for two age brackets of boys and girls, but also opening up opportunities for educational scholarships at some of the top colleges throughout the country.

It costs $75 to join and kids can play in several non-invitational events during the year. They get a subscription to *Golf Week* magazine, a regular newsletter from the association, a calendar, a bag tag, the official *Rules of Golf*, and a listing of which events determine AJGA Junior All-American status.

There is also a CBS (college bound student) membership. In addition to the above, it includes the *PING American College Golf Guide*, and the *AJGA Player Profile Service*. This is sent to college golf coaches around the country and profiles the member, which may be you! They also have access to important college golf resource information.

Of particular importance here is that the association has built a reputation among junior golfers and college coaches which results in many of the coaches coming to the events to get a "pulse" on the aspiring student-golfers. *If you're a good golfer,*

have good grades, and the right attitude, you may end up with a
college scholarship.

Not all of the following names were great players when they
entered AJGA, but they got a great college education, with
scholarship, and became pretty good players . . . people like
Brandie Burton, David Duval, Billy Mayfair, Trip Kuehne, Phil
Michelson, Michelle McGann, Scott Verplank, Kelly Kuehne,
Justin Leonard and . . . who was that other one? . . . oh, Tiger
Woods!

AJGA is located at:
1980 Sports Club Drive
Braselton, GA 30517

Or call toll free:
1-877-373-2542

The 16th Tee:
Great Golf Books

In the past few years, I've added to my collection of golf books (by the way, I'm not a collector . . . it just "happened") five that stand out not as golf books, but as *good* books.

Every Shot I Take by Davis Love III.

It's a simple story exuding the love of father for son, and the respect of son for father. While there is much to be learned about playing the game, it is told in such a way that it is more than a series of lessons in golf; it is truly enjoyable, and memorable . . . if you like "family" you'll like this.

Follow the Wind by Bo Links.

This is a fascinating story—no, a fantasy—about a young man who plays golf at Lincoln Park in San Francisco (the course is real). He hits an errant shot which leads him through a misty "enclave" where he comes upon Ben Hogan, and subsequently Walter Hagen and Francis Ouimet and even Bobby Jones. This book is for any golfer, of any age.

Final Rounds by Jim Dodson.

What a wonderful story, and it is Jim's. He takes his father back to where the game started and environs. They relive the father's experiences in the UK during World War II. They are fascinating, and of course, emotional because Jim is in fact on a "final round" with his dad, who is terminally ill with cancer. They play many of the courses the elder Dodson had played in his earlier "visit" to "the auld country." But it's no "downer." When you get to the end of the book, you'll feel good too! I know I did, and so did my sons, each of whom I gave a copy.

To The Linksland by Michael Bamberger.
Maybe my favorite. It's Bamberger's story of Bamberger's love of golf. A high school and college golf nut . . . only a fairly good player . . . i.e., mid 70s on a good day. After college he still agonizes over playing golf, over "there." Quits his newspaper job, convinces his new wife "this is the time" and off they trudge to Europe, and he pays the "freight" by caddying on the European Tour. Their adventures on the tour are only the beginning. He finally gets to St. Andrews, and then . . . well, then it gets into a wonderful story of playing the old course—badly—and meeting a wonderful old professional who enhances Bamberger's gratification of finally learning why it is that he loves the game so much, and why its traditions sharpen his appetite for it. One of its most memorable lines emerges after a round of golf, at a very special and "hidden away" course with his new friend, the old professional, when this new mentor says to him, "the difference between Scottish Golfers and Americans is . . . we play to enjoy the game, you play to win it." And of course the reader can read what he chooses into that thought.

The Greatest Player That Never Lived by Michael Vernon.
As you read the beginnings of this book you feel you're reading a newspaper story. *(maybe you are).* Then, a bit further along a mystery story. *(Maybe you are.)* In any case, you'll find it difficult to turn the light off, for here is a story built around Bobby Jones as one of the two central characters. You find yourself saying you never knew all this about Jones, and of course, you didn't because it's fiction, but that's hard to believe. *(Or is it?)* You'll experience frustration, compassion, and gratification; it's *really* great. I've read a lot of sports books and enjoyed most of them, but I have never before experienced the kinds of emotions these golf books made me feel.

The Road to Ballybunion by John deGarmo.

What can I say about my own book beyond telling you it has a few surprises? It's all about courses and Irish caddie humor, and even some of the history and culture at these County Kerry (southwest Ireland) sites. Lots of photographs and paintings for those of you who like golf photography and paintings!

If, after reading a selection, or all of these, your appreciation for golf isn't greater than before, I'd be very surprised. But just as important, is that your appreciation for story telling will be gratified, too.

I've read a lot of sports books and enjoyed most of them, but I have never before experienced the kinds of emotions these golf books made me feel.

I'm reasonably sure there must be some others that may be as good . . . but I haven't seen them.

The 17th Tee:
Rules and Integrity

The most impressive words I've ever heard, relating integrity to the game of golf, came from Robert T. Jones. When someone commended him for calling a stroke penalty on himself, he said:

"A person might as well praise a man for not robbing a bank."

These words say just about everything that can possibly be said about maintaining an unflinching, inflexible, unyielding commitment to the rules of *the greatest game of all . . .*

WITHOUT RULES . . . IT'S JUST <u>NOT</u> A GAME

My experience with the rules of this game is that they are truly logical. They were written to help you, not to hinder you. There may be times when you might challenge this, but believe me, the more you play by the rules, the more you'll agree.

Because the rules at times can seem a bit complicated, you'll see on the following pages excerpts we have taken from the USGA's *Golf Rules in Brief*—those rules that we think you might need most at this point in learning the game. These are reprinted here with the permission of The United States Golf Association.

We believe that you'll have few problems if you simply play the ball as it lies, and the course as you find it. If you find yourself unable to do either, do what is fair; that's the principle of the rules.

USGA Golf Rules In Brief

A summary of some principal Rules of Golf. In case of doubt, refer to the complete rules published by the United States Golf Association and the Royal and Ancient Golf Club of St. Andrews.

The following excerpts from *Golf Rules in Brief* are reprinted with the permission of the United States Golf Association.

Etiquette

1. Don't move, talk or stand close to or directly behind a player making a stroke.
2. Don't play until the group in front is out of the way.
3. Always play without delay. Leave the putting green as soon as all players in your group have holed out.
4. Invite faster groups to play through.
5. Repair divot holes. Smooth out footprints in bunkers.
6. Don't step on the line of another's putt.
7. Don't drop clubs on a putting green.
8. Replace the flagstick carefully in an upright position.
9. Leave the course in the condition in which you'd like to find it.

Match and Stroke Play

1. Put an identification mark on your ball. If you can't identify it as yours, it's lost. (27) If your ball becomes unfit for play, you may replace it, without penalty, on the hole where it becomes unfit or between holes. (5-3)
2. Count your clubs. No more than 14. (4-4)
3. Don't use an artificial device or unusual equipment for gauging or measuring distance or conditions, or to give artificial aid in gripping. (14-3)
4. Don't ask for advice from anyone except your partner or your caddie. Don't give advice to anyone except your partner. (8-1)

5. During a hole you may practice swing but not play a practice stroke. Between holes you may practice chip and put it on or near the putting green of the hole last played or the tee of the next hole but not from a hazard. (7-2)

6. Play without delay. (6-7)

Order of Play

1. On the first tee, the honor is determined by the order of the draw or, in absence of a draw, by lot. (10)

2. In match play, the ball farther from the hole is played first. The winner of a hole tees off first on the next hole. If a player plays out of turn anywhere on the course, his opponent may require him to replay. (10-1)

3. In stroke play, the ball farthest from the hole is played first. The competitor with the lowest score on a hole tees off first on the next hole. There is generally no penalty for playing out of turn. (10-2)

4. In four-ball competitions, partners may play in the order they consider best. (30-3c and 31-5)

Teeing Ground

1. Tee off within two club-lengths behind the front edges of the tee-markers.

2. If you tee off outside this area, in match play there is no penalty but your opponent may require you to replay the stroke. In stroke play you incur a two-stroke penalty and must then play from within the proper area. (11-4)

Playing the Ball

1. Play the ball as it lies. (13-1) Don't touch it unless a Rule permits. (18-2)

2. Play the course as you find it. Don't improve your lie, the area of your intended stance or swing or your line of play or a reasonable extension of that line beyond the hole by moving, bending or breaking anything fixed or growing except in fairly taking your stance or making your swing. Don't press anything down. (13-2) Don't build a stance. (13-3)

3. If your ball is in a bunker or a water hazard, don't touch the ground in the bunker or the ground or water in the water hazard before the downswing. (13-4)
4. Strike at the ball with the clubhead. Don't push or scrape it. (14-1) If your club strikes the ball more than once in a single stroke, count the stroke and add a penalty stroke. (14-4)
5. If you play a wrong ball (except in a hazard), in match play you lose the hole. In stroke play you incur a two-stroke penalty and must then play the correct ball. (15)

Putting Green

1. Don't touch the line of your putt unless a Rule permits. (16-1a) You may repair ball marks and old hole plugs on the line but not spike marks. (16-1c)
2. You may lift, and if desired clean, your ball on the putting green. Always replace it on the exact spot. (16-1b)
3. Don't test the surface face by scraping it or rolling a ball. (16-1d)
4. If your ball played from the putting green strikes the flagstick, in match play you lose the hole or in stroke play you incur a two-stroke penalty. (17-3)
5. Always hole out unless in match play your opponent concedes your putt. (2-4, 3-2, 16-2)

Ball at Rest Moved

1. If your ball is moved by you, your partner or your caddie except as permitted by the Rules or if it moves after you have addressed it, add a penalty stroke and replace your ball. (18-2)
2. If your ball is moved by someone else or another ball, replace it, without penalty to you. (18)

Ball in Motion Deflected or Stopped

1. If your ball in motion is deflected or stopped by you, your partner or your caddie, in match play you lose the

hole. In stroke play you incur a two-stroke penalty and the ball is played as it lies. (19-2)

2. If your ball in motion is deflected or stopped by someone else, play your ball as it lies without penalty, except (a) in match play, if an opponent or his caddie deflects your ball, you may play it as it lies or replay it or (b) in stroke play, if your ball is deflected after a stroke on the putting green, you must replay. (19)

3. If your ball in motion is deflected or stopped by another ball in play and at rest, play your ball as it lies. In match play, you incur no penalty. In stroke play, you incur a two-stroke penalty if your ball and the other ball were on the green before your stroke. (19-5)

Lifting, Dropping and Placing

1. If a ball to be lifted is to be replaced (e.g., when the ball is lifted on the putting green to clean it), its position must be marked. (20-1)

2. When dropping, stand erect. hold the ball at shoulder height and arm's length and drop it. A ball to be dropped in a hazard must be dropped, and stay, in the hazard. (20-2a)

3. If a dropped ball strikes the player or his partner, caddie or equipment, it must be re-dropped without penalty. (20-2a)

4. A dropped ball must be re-dropped if it rolls into a hazard, out of a hazard, onto a putting green, out of bounds or to a position where there is interference by the condition from which relief is taken (in case of immovable obstructions, abnormal ground conditions, embedded ball and wrong putting green) or comes to rest more than two club-lengths from where it first struck a part of the course or nearer the hole than its original position, nearest point of relief under Rules 24 and 25 or where the ball last crossed the water hazard margin under Rule 26-1. If the ball when re-dropped rolls into any position listed above, place it where it first struck a part of the course when re-dropped. (20-2c)

5. If the original lie of a ball to be replaced has been altered, place it in the nearest similar lie within one club-length not nearer the hole, except in a bunker recreate the original lie and place it in that lie. (20-3b)

Ball Interfering with or Assisting Play

1. You may lift your ball if it might assist any other player. (22)
2. You may have any other ball lifted if it might interfere with your play or assist any other player. (22)

Loose Impediments

1. Loose impediments are natural objects (such as stones and leaves) not fixed or growing, not solidly embedded and not adhering to the ball. (23)
2. You may move them unless the loose impediment and your ball lie in or touch the same hazard. (23-1)
3. If you move a loose impediment within one club-length of your ball and your ball moves, the ball must be replaced and (unless your ball was on the putting green) you incur a penalty stroke. (18-2c)

Obstructions

1. Obstructions are artificial (i.e., man made) objects. Objects defining out of bounds such as fence posts or stakes and immovable artificial objects out of bounds are not obstructions. (24)
2. Movable obstructions (e.g., a rake) anywhere may be moved. If your ball moves, replace it without penalty. (24-1)
3. If an immovable obstruction (e.g., a water fountain) interferes with your stance or swing, you may, except when your ball is in water hazard, drop within one club-length of the nearest point of relief not nearer the hole. In a bunker drop in the bunker, and on the putting green place in the nearest position which affords relief, not nearer the hole. There is no relief for intervention on your line of play unless your ball and the obstructions are on the green. (24-2)

4. If your ball is lost in an immovable obstruction (except when the entrance is in a water hazard) take the same relief based on the point where the ball entered the obstruction. (24-2c)

Abnormal Ground Conditions

1. If your ball is in an abnormal ground condition (casual water, ground under repair, a hole, cast or runway made by a burrowing animal) you may drop without penalty within one club-length of the nearest point of relief not nearer the hole, except (a) in a bunker drop in the bunker or (b) on the putting green place at the nearest point of relief. (25-1b)

2. If you ball is lost in an abnormal ground condition (except in a water hazard), take the same relief based on the point where the ball last crossed the margin of the area. (25-1c)

Water Hazards

1. You may play the ball as it lies or, under penalty of one stroke, drop any distance behind the water hazard keeping the point at which the original ball last crossed the margin of the water hazard directly between the hole and the spot on which the ball is dropped, or replay the shot. (26-1a,b)

2. In a lateral water hazard, you may also, under penalty of one stroke, drop within two club-lengths of (a) the point where the ball last crossed the hazard margin or (b) a point on the opposite hazard margin equidistant from the hole. (26-1c)

Lost or Out of Bounds

1. If your ball may be lost outside a water hazard or out of bounds, you may play a provisional ball before you go forward to look for the original, provided you announce your intention to do so. If your original ball turns out to be in a water hazard or is found outside a water hazard, you must abandon the provisional ball. (27-2)

2. If your ball is lost outside a water hazard or is out of bounds, add one penalty stroke and play the provisional or, if you did not play a provisional, replay the shot. (27-1)

Unplayable

If you believe your ball is unplayable outside a water hazard you may add one penalty stroke and (a) drop within two club-lengths of where the ball lies not nearer the hole, (b) drop any distance behind the point where the ball lay (keeping that point directly between the hole and the spot on which the ball is dropped), or (c) replay the shot. If your ball is in a bunker you may proceed under (a), (b), or (c), however, if you elect to proceed under (a) or (b), you must drop in the bunker. (28)

Rex is taking a drop in the right manner.

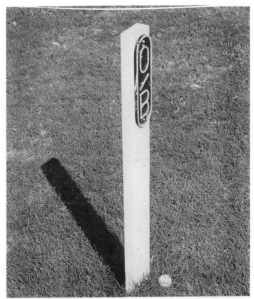

Out of bounds stakes aren't artificial, so you can't move them.
And you can't move the ball without a penalty stroke.

Rex is teed up fine—behind the markers, and within two club lengths of them.

This obstruction is not movable, so Rex gets a free drop.

It isn't covered in what we've selected from the rules book, but just so you know, the player taking relief (from the cart path) must take total relief, which is why Greg's brother Will is pointing that out to him (get both feet off the path!)

Brianna, Will, Greg, and Rex

Just picture this on a sports page headline, in 2015:

One Lady and Two Brothers Lead at Whistling Straits; Only Six Players Under Par with One Round to Go

In only the third U.S. Open where men and women compete against each other from the same tees, three golfers from the southeast U.S. are setting the pace at this great western course, holding its second U.S. Open in the past six years.

Brianna Walker, a 26-year-old all around athlete from Sawgrass in Ponte Vedra, Florida birdied the last three holes for her third straight 70 and a two stroke lead over the 25-year-old Kennedy Twins, also from Ponte Vedra.

The Kennedy brothers, Will and Greg, are in at 212. They are the same two that cleaned up in the NCAA's in 2010, and then won the U.S. Amateur, Greg in 2010, and Will in 2011. In both amateurs they played against each other in the 36 hole finals, going three extra holes both times.

At 214 is Rex LeBlond, a thirty-year-old business man golfer and winner of this years Metropolitan Amateur Championship, played at famed Winged Foot.

Golfer's News

page 3

. . . And now back to reality . . .

Fantasy? Maybe. Possibility? Who knows. In any case these are our models for this book; let me tell you a bit about them.

Brianna is 11 years old at this writing. She is truly an all around athlete—a superb swimmer, tennis player and even a dancer. Brianna also is a top level student at a local school, which gives her ample time to practice her swing; and the pictures in our book show she knows what she's doing.

The Kennedy boys, Will and Greg, are 10 years old. In addition to golf they both play soccer; they both play tennis; they both swim and they're both lucky to have a built-in person right at home to compete with. And yes, they too are excellent students. Both have already had a natural birdie—in just their third year at golf.

And there's Rex LeBlond, the 15-year-old senior member of our model panel. Rex attends Fordham Prep in New York City, where he gets excellent grades in academia and excels on both the basketball and baseball teams.

What fun they've been to work with!

Brianna Walker

Will and Greg Kennedy

William P. Kennedy   *Gregory T. Kennedy*

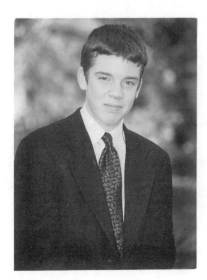

Rex LeBlond

Richard LeBlond IV

The 18th Tee:
Final Thoughts

Golf is very simply a game that far transcends any sport that requires athletic activity.

Golf has that magical mystique which embraces all the emotions and most of the verities we're confronted with, and experience in our day-to-day living. Think about it; golf's promises fulfilled, can result in gratifications we almost inevitably don't believe can happen. Golf's mistakes often result in generating Herculean disciplines at the practice tee and green; disciplines most of us didn't really know we had.

Golf's participants, whether they kid each other, needle each other, encourage each other or congratulate each other, inevitably form a bond to the game and to each other. What game do you know of, where these almost conflicting modes and moods exist?

What game do you know of where humor and pathos and philosophy and integrity, and sportsmanship and mentorship all are part of the game?

Golf is a game without dimensions. It, like space, appears to have no periphery.

FORE ...

John de Tarmo

When the going gets tough, the tough get going.
—Robert Kennedy
U.S. Attorney General

Truths About Golf

Chances are you'll never be as good as you hope to be if you change your swing with every new idea that someone has about the golf swing.

Watch The Masters on TV and you'll learn more strategy about approach shots to greens than if you read 50 books about it.

When Arnold Palmer says the roles of integrity and dress code should remain intact . . . they should remain intact.

Tell your Mom and Dad and instructor to never let you get away from fundamentals. Never.

Golf is like a butterfly; it hovers around you . . . you think you've got it, and then it gets away, but it will be back.

You may think you know what your swing looks like, but nothing knows as well as a camera; photos often talk better than words.

Three different teachers aren't three times better than one.

If at the top of your backswing your club is pointing at the target, chances are your shot will be mighty close to target.

You don't have to have a perfect swing to enjoy the game—besides, nobody has one.

A putt well struck, though missed, is very nearly as enjoyable as one that's made . . . think about it.

There are more winners in golf than heroes. That's 'cause winners are usually smarter about their shots than those who would be heroes.

APPENDIX:

Golf Digest's
Summer Golf Camps

FOR ALL AGES, FOR BEGINNERS AND ALL LEVELS OF COMPETENCE, THROUGHOUT THE U.S.A. WITH TWO IN SCOTLAND.

There are approximately one hundred golf camps listed here. These were provided by *Golf Digest*. The list has camps for every level of experience and includes periods from one day to four weeks.

The overwhelming majority of these "teaching centers" have been providing excellent instructional help for many years. Their staffs include PGA and LPGA professionals, as well as college golf coaches.

While some details are not listed, we have in almost every case given phone numbers, addresses, and email addresses. You may use these for further information; you might even wish to reach *Golf Digest* via the Internet, at *GolfDigest.com.*

We wish you well.

Camps in the NORTHEAST

Birch Run/Adelphia Golf Camp
Birch Run C.C., Birch Run Rd, Allegany,
NY 14706, ph: 716 373-3113
one 3-day summer session: $150

FCA Junior Golf Camps
P.O. Box 664, Ponte Vedra Beach, FL
32004, ph: 904 273-9541
one 4-day summer session,
Green Mountain G.C.,
Killington, VT: $535

Foster's Golf Camp
240 Tory Rd., Manchester, NH 03104
ph: 603-622-1553
1-week summer session: $225; day camp

**Links at Hiawatha Landing
Junior Golf Camps**
2350 Marshland Rd./P.O. Box 451,
Apalachin, NY 13732, ph: 607 687-6952,
www.hiawathalinks.com
nine 5-day summer sessions: $100-$125;
day camp

Maine Golf Academy
2720 Taylor Woods Rd., Belgrade, ME
04917, ph: 888 465-3226,
www.golfcamp.com
two-week sessions: $2,595
four-week sessions: $4,495

Nike Jr. Golf Camps
919 Sir Francis Drake Blvd., Kentfield,
CA 94904, ph: 800 645-3226,
us-sportscamps.com
various locations and dates for resident golf

(Nike Jr. cont.)
camps: Williams College, MA.; Stowe C.C.,
NY; Loomis Chaffee, CT; Yale Univ., CT;
Mount Snow, VT; Sugarloaf G.C.,
Carrabassett, ME; Links at Hiawatha
Landing, Apalachin, NY; $875-$1,275.

Offense-Defense Golf Camp
P.O. Box 6, Easton, CT 06612
ph: 800 824-7336; 203 256-9844
www.offensedefensegolf.com
one- to three-week summer sessions:
$865 (board), $495 (day)

PGA Jr. Golf School
Metropolitan Section, 49 Knollwood Rd,
Ste. 200, Elmsford, NY 10523
ph: 914 347-2416 , *www.pga.org*
two summer sessions: $175 for associ-
ation members; $200 for nonmembers

Sugarloaf Golf Club
Junior Golf Camp
Box 5000, Carrabassett Valley, ME 04947
ph: 207 237-6812, *www.sugarloaf.com*
one-week summer sessions: $769

Young Executive Golf Camps
P.O. Box 16242, Hooksett, NH 03106
ph: 603 669-8031
www.youngexecsgolfcamp.com
weeklong summer day sessions: $220

Camps in the
MID-ATLANTIC

Bob Benning Future Stars School
35271 Prestwick Court, Round Hill,
VA 20141, ph: 703 589-1443,
www.benningolf.com
three-day summer sessions: $240

Coaches Golf School at Purdue
Purdue University, 1586 Stewart Center,
Rm. 110, West Lafayette, IN 47907
ph: 765 496-3935
www.coachesgolfschool.com
three 4-day summer sessions: $1,090

FCA Junior Golf Camps
P.O. Box 664, Ponte Vedra Beach, FL
32004, ph: 904 273-9541, *www.fcagolf.org*

(FCA cont.)
three summer sessions: Eagle Creek
G.C., Indianapolis; Longaberger G.C.,
Penn State Univ.; $425-$495

Fighting Scot Golf Camp
College of Wooster, Wooster, OH 44691
ph: 330 263-2170
two 4-day summer sessions: $575

4 Star Summer Camps
P.O. Box 3387, Falls Church, VA 22043
ph: 800 334-7827, *www.4starcamps.com*
various 3-day sessions: $795

Foresite Golf Clinics
632 Germantown Pike, Lafayette Hill, PA
19444, ph: 888 882-5440
www.foresitesports.com
5-day summer sessions, June-Aug: $165;
day camp

Green's Folly Golf Camp
Green's Folly G. Cse., 1085 Green's Folly
Rd., South Boston, VA 24592
ph: 800 337-4998, *www.greensfolly.com*
three 4-day summer sessions: $495

Murray State Golf School
Murray State Univesrity
223 Stewart Stadium
Murray, KY 42071
ph: 270 762-5408
one 5-day summer session: $400

Nike Golf Camps
919 Sir Francis Drake Blvd, Kentfield,
CA 94904, ph: 800 645-3226
us-sportscamps.com
various locations and dates for resident
camps: Rutgers Univ., NJ; Lawrenceville,
NJ; Shawnee Inn, PA; Kutztown Univ., PA;
Oglebay, WV; Univ. of Maryland; Univ. of
Virginia; Williamsburg/Kingsmill, VA;
Dayton, OH; Notre Dame, IN; Akron, OH;
N. Kentucky Univ: $875-$1,125

Penn State Golf Camps
Penn State University, 204 Multi-Sport
Facility, University Park, PA 16802
ph: 814 865-0561
www.sportcamps.outreach.psu.edu
five 4-day summer sessions

PGM Golf Clinics
P.O. Box 27531, Philadelphia, PA 19118
ph: 215 247-3821
weekly summer sessions: $200 per week

Stoneleigh Jr. Camp
35271 Prestwick Court, Round Hill, VA
20141, ph: 703 859-1402
www.stoneleighgolf.com
one 3-day summer session: $100; day
camp

Tom Hanna Jr. Playing Camp
22611 Indian Point Rd., Bozman, MD
21612, ph: 301 403-8157,
www.hannagolf.com
four 4-day summer sessions: $950

University Jr. Golf Camp
University of Maryland, University Blvd.,
College Park, MD 20740, ph: 301 403-
4299, *www.inform.umd.edu*
two 4-day summer sessions

Camps in the
SOUTH

Academy of Golf Dynamics
45 Club Estates Pkwy, Austin, TX 78738,
ph: 800 879-2008, *www.golfdynamics.com*
3-day sessions, June-Sept: $750

Arnold Palmer Golf Academy
Saddlebrook Resort, 5700 Saddlebrook
Way, Wesley Chapel, FL 33543
ph: 800 729-8383 ext. 4653
www.golf-academy.com
year-round: $995-$1,295 per week

Auburn Tiger Golf Camp
P.O. Box 351, Auburn, AL 36831
ph: 334 844-9759
one 4-day summer session: $600 (board),
$450 (day)

Camp Olympia Jr. Golf Academy
Rte. 2, Box 25-B, Trinity, TX 75862
ph: 936 594-2541, *www.campolympia.com*
four 2-week summer sessions: $2,120
(two weeks), $2,745 (three weeks)

Campbell University Golf School
P.O. Box 10, Buies Creek, NC 27506
ph: 910 893-1401, *www.campbell.edu*
two 4-day summer sessions: $550

Crimson Tide Golf Academy
16053 Carmel Bay Dr.
Northport, AL 35406
ph: 205 348-0383, *www.roll.tide.ua.edu*
three weekly summer sessions: $650-$795

David Leadbetter Jr. Golf Camps
5500 34th St. West, Bradenton, FL 34210
ph: 941 739-2483, 800 872-6425
year-round sessions: $1,200 (board),
$1,000 (day)

Duke Academy of Golf
Duke Golf Club, P.O. Box 90552
Durham, NC 27708, ph: 919 681-2628
two summer sessions: $1,125

Duke Golf School
P.O. Box 90551, Durham, NC 27708
ph: 919 681-2494, *www.goduke.com*
two summer sessions

FCA Jr. Golf Camps
P.O. Box 664, Ponte Vedra Beach, FL
32004, ph: 904 273-9541, *www.fcagolf.org*
six locations: $425-$775

Georgia Tech Golf Camp
205 Park Creek Dr., Alpharetta, GA
30005, ph: 404 894-0961
one 5-day summer session: $850

Golf Schools at Wild Dunes
5757 Palm Blvd., Isle of Palms, SC 29451
ph: 843 886-2022
daily clinics, June-Aug: $20 per day

Grand Cypress Jr. Golf Academy
One North Jacaranda, Orlando, FL 32836
ph: 407 239-1975
www.grandcypress.com
5-day summer sessions: $330; day camp

Hank Haney Golf Ranch Jr.
Development Camps, 4104 Custer Rd.
McKinne, TX 75070,
ph: 972 529-2221
eleven 4-day sessions, March-July: $275

Innisbrook Troon Golf Jr. Institute
Westin Innisbrook Resort, 36750 U.S.
Hwy. 19 N., Palm Harbor, FL 34684
www.westininnisbrook.com
various sessions: $575

International Junior Golf Academy
7 Office Park Rd., Ste. 105
Hilton Head, SC 29938
ph: 843 785-4540, *www.ijga.com*
weeklong sessions throughout the year

Jerry Haas Golf Camp
Wake Forest University, P.O. Box 7567
Winston-Salem, NC 27109
ph: 336 758-6000
weeklong summer sessions: $1,100

Jim McLean Golf School
Doral Resort, 4400 N.W. 87th Ave.
Miami, FL 33178
ph: 305 591-6409, *www.jimmclean.com*
5-day summer sessions

**Jim Suttie's Florida Gulf Coast
University Jr. Camp**
10501 FGCU Blvd. South, Ft. Myers, FL
33965, ph: 940 590-7012, *www.fgcu.edu*
summer sessions

Longhorn Jr. Golf Camp
University of Texas, P.O. Box 7399
Austin, TX 78713, ph: 512 471-3167
www.texassports.com
summer sessions: $850

Massengale/Olson Golf Academy
2301 N. Millbend, The Woodlands, TX
77380, ph: 281 292-4653
www.massengale/olsongolfacademy.com
six summer sessions: $145-$375

Mic Potter Golf Schools at Furman
3300 Poinsett Hwy, Greenvile, SC 29613
ph: 864 294-6283
four summer sessions: $285 (day); $850
(board); $170 (mini-day)

Mike Holder Golf Camp
Oklahoma State Univ., Gallagher-Iba
Arena, Stillwater, OK 74078
ph: 405 269-0726
two summer sessions: $900

Nike Jr. Golf Camps
919 Sir Francis Drake Blvd
Kentfield, CA 94904
ph: 800 645-3226, *us-sportscamps.com*
various locations and dates

**North Carolina State Wolfpack
Golf School**
3000 Ballybunion Way, Raleigh, NC
27613, ph: 919 846-1536
three summer sessions: $205-$390; day
camps

Ole Miss Golf Camp
Univ. of Mississippi, Athletic West,
Fraternity Row, University, MS 38677
ph: 662 915-7581, *www.olemiss.edu*
two summer sessions

Pine Needles Youth Golfari
P.O. Box 88, Southern Pines, NC 28387
ph: 910 692-7111
www.pineneedles-midpines.com
two summer sessions: $1,695

Pinehurst Jr. Golf Advantage School
P.O. Box 4000, Pinehurst Resort & C.C.
Pinehurst, NC 28374
ph: 800 795-4653 ext. 5
eight summer sessions: $1,335-$1,435

**R.T. Jones Golf Trail
Academy of Golf Jr. Program**
167 Sun Belt Pkwy, Birmingham, AL
35211, ph: 800 949-4444 ext. 353
www.rtjgolf.com
4-day summer sessions: $200

Tar Heel Golf School
P.O. Box 3282, Chapel Hill, NC 27515
ph: 919 402-1034
www.tarheelgolfschool.com
three summer sesions: $950

Tennessee PGA Jr. Golf Academy
400 Franklin Rd., Franklin, TN 37069
ph: 615 790-3336
www.golfhousetennessee.com
ten summer sessions

**Texas A&M John Jacobs Jr.
Golf School**
c/o Athletic Dept., Texas A&M, College
Station, TX 77843, ph: 979 845-4533
three summer sessions: $650

Top Gun Jr. Golf Academy
16641 La Cantera Pkwy., San Antonio,
TX 78256, ph: 888 603-4653
four sessions: $1,249 (board), $799 (day)

TTA Teen Golf Tour
1121 Holland Dr., Ste. 21, Boca Raton,
FL 33487, ph: 888 868-7882
www.ttateengolftour.com
one 3-week session: $5,495

**University of South Carolina
Junior Golf School**
1300 Rosewood Dr., Columbia, SC 29208
ph: 803 777-7054, *www.uscsports.com*
one session: $850

Walt Disney World Jr. Golf Camp
P.O. Box 10000, Lake Buena Vista, FL
32830, ph: 407 938-3435
six summer sessions: $250

Camps in the MIDWEST

Boyne National Jr. Golf Academy
1 Boyne Mountain Rd., Boyne Falls, MI
49713, ph: 231 549-6001, *www.boyne.com*
eight summer sessions: $675

Cyclone Golf Camp
Iowa State University, Jacobsen Athletic
Bldg, Ames, IA 50011, ph: 515 294-3823
www.cyclones.com
two summer sessions: $449

Falcon Golf Camp
U.S. Air Force Academy, Dept. of
Athletics, Bldg. 2169, Colorado Springs,
CO 80840, ph: 719 333-2280
www.airforcesports.com
two summer sessions: $825

FCA Golf Camps
P.O. Box 664, Ponte Vedra Beach, FL
32004, ph: 904 273-9541, *www.fcagolf.com*
seven summer sessions

**Gongaware Indiana Junior
Golf Academy**
2625 N. Hurricane Rd., Franklin, IN 46131
ph: 800 779-7271, *www.indianagolf.com*

Iowa PGA Jr. Golf
1930 St. Andrews Ct. NE, Cedar Rapids,
IA 52402, ph: 319 378-9142
www.iowagolf.com
one summer session: $395

Jayhawk Golf Camp
2104 Inverness Dr., Lawrence, KS 66047
ph: 785 842-1907, -1714
two summer sessions: $700

McGetrick Golf Academy
9742 S. Meridian Blvd., Englewood, CO
80112, ph: 303 799-0870
www.mcgetrickgolf.com
one summer session: $550

Minnesota Golf Instructional Camp
P.O. Box 13130
Minneapolis, MN 55414
ph: 612 625-5863
www.mngolfcomp.com
four summer sessions: $445 (day), $545
(advanced)

Minnesota PGA Jr. Golf
12800 Bunker Prairie Rd., Coon Rapids,
MN 55448, ph: 763 754-6641
1-day camps, June-Aug: $80 per day
2-day academy: $160

Nike Jr. Golf Camps
919 Sir Francis Drake Blvd.
Kentfield, CA 94904
ph: 800 645-3226
various locations and dates for resident golf
camps: Boulder, CO; SO Illinois Univ.; Lake
Geneva, WI; SentryWorld, WI; Aspen, CO;
Western Ill. Univ.; St. John's, MN;
Springfield, MO; Michigan State Univ.;
Ferris State Univ., MI; Kansas State Univ.:
$550-$995

Rob Hary Jr. Golf Academy
6300 Auto Club Rd., Bloomington, MN
55438, ph: 952 884-1744
three summer sessions (mornings only):
$135

Silver Sands Golf Academy
P.O. Box 1268, Lake Geneva, WI 53147
ph: 800 232-1834
www.silversandsgolf.com
eight summer sessions: $699-$875

Camps in the WEST

Bull Durham Jr. Golf
2351 Hamilton Rd., Alamogordo NM
88310, ph: 505 437-02290
one summer session: $500

Championship G. Cse. Jr. Golf School
UNM G. Cse., Albuquerque, NM 87131
ph: 505 277-4546
one summer session: $60; day camp

FCA Jr. Golf Camps
P.O. Box 664
Ponte Vedra Beach, FL 32004
ph: 904 273-9541, *www.fcagolf.com*
one summer session: Powder Horn,
Sheridan, WY, $485

Sun Devil Golf Camp at Arizona State Univ.
Box 872505, Stadium Dr., Tempe, AZ
85287, ph: 480 965-4277
two sessions: $800

Top Gun Golf Academy
2351 Hamilton Rd., Alamogordo, NM,
88310, ph: 505 437-0290
one session for advance players: $500

UCLA Golf Camp
P.O. Box 24044, Los Angeles, CA 90024
ph: 310 206-3550, *www.uclabruins.com*
one session: $995

INTERNATIONAL CAMPS

Grass Roots Golf
12 Bank St.
Glasgow, Scotland G12 8JQ
ph: 011-44-141-357-3438
www.grassrootsgolf.com
four 6-day sessions at St. Andrews: $938
two sessions at Sterling: $788

Nike Jr. Golf Camps
919 Sir Francis Drake Blvd
Kentfield, CA 94904
ph: 800 645-3226, *us-sportscamps.com*
one summer session: St. Andrews,
Scotland (advanced): $3,495, incl. airfare

About the Authors

John deGarmo, Author

John deGarmo has made his *avocation* his *vocation*. An aspiring golfer from his pre-teen years, he played high school and college golf. After the war years he dabbled in regional competitive events, according to him with no great success, though his shelves would tend to belie that.

After a career in advertising in New York City, deGarmo "retired" into golf. He worked with the American Junior Golf Association and served as chairman of its Advisory Board. DeGarmo also became involved in golf residential marketing and then began his career as a writer. He co-authored *The Spirit of Golf,* illustrated by impressionist painter Ray Ellis, and *The Road to Ballybunion,* which takes its readers through a delightful smorgasbord of southwest Ireland's cultural, anecdotal, and historical tidbits, of course seasoned with six of the country's famous and not-so-famous golf courses.

Sam Wiley, Co-Author

Co-author Sam Wiley is presently a PGA Head Professional at Wee Burn Country Club in Darien, Connecticut. His reputation has developed with a series of successful stints, first as an assistant professional at Fox Chapel in Pittsburgh, Pennsylvania; Canoe Brook in Summit, New Jersey; Oak Hill in Rochester, New York; and Caves Valley in Baltimore, Maryland.

Prior to Wiley's selection as Head Professional at Wee Burn, he spent three years as Head Professional at the Country Club of Buffalo. During the off-season in northern climes, Wiley worked as as instructor in Florida with the highly acclaimed Jim McClean golf schools. While there, he had the unique and gratifying experience of working with Paul Azinger when Azinger was preparing for his return to the PGA Tour.

There isn't a football channel,
or a basketball channel,
or a baseball channel,
or a ping-pong channel;
no, in this whole world of sport . . .
there's only a golf channel.
That kind of tells you something.